3.

'Traditional Food East and West of the Pennines'

'Traditional Food East and West of the Pennines'

Papers by
Peter Brears, Lynette Hunter,
Helen Pollard, Jennifer Stead and
C. Anne Wilson

EDITED BY C. ANNE WILSON

with illustrations by
Peter Brears

Edinburgh University Press

Papers from the Third Leeds Symposium
on Food History and Traditions,
April 1988, with additional papers

© C. Anne Wilson, 1991
Edinburgh University Press
22 George Square, Edinburgh

Typeset in Alphacomp Garamond
by Pioneer Associates Limited, Perthshire, and
printed in Great Britain by
Page Bros Ltd, Norwich

British Library Cataloguing
in Publication Data

Traditional food east and west of the Pennines.
- (Food and society series)
I. Wilson, Anne C.   II. Series
641.3009427

ISBN 0 7486 0118 X (cased)

Contents

Contents

About the Contributors

PETER BREARS is the Director of Leeds City Museums. He combines his interests in archaeology, architecture and the traditional food of Northern England with a great deal of practical experience of recreating the culinary confections of earlier centuries. His publications include *The Gentlewoman's Kitchen: Great Food in Yorkshire 1650-1750*, and *Traditional Food in Yorkshire*.

LYNETTE HUNTER is a Senior Lecturer at the University of Leeds' Institute of Bibliography and Textual Criticism. She has published several books and articles on modern English literature, and is general editor of *Household and Cookery Books Published in Britain* 1800-1914.

HELEN POLLARD has taught home economics at Bury and, more recently, as Head of Home Economics at Kirbie Kendal School. She has both written and spoken on radio programmes about traditional Lancashire foods. She is interested in all aspects of food and nutrition in Britain, and has built up an extensive collection of British cookery books.

JENNIFER STEAD trained as an art historian and writes on social history and food history. Her publications include *Food and Cooking in 18th Century Britain*.

ANNE WILSON has worked for many years in the Brotherton Library of the University of Leeds, becoming involved in food history as a result of cataloguing the John Preston Collection of early English cookery books. Her publications include *Food and Drink in Britain from the Stone Age to Recent Times* and *The Book of Marmalade*. She is currently researching the very early history of distilling.

List of illustrations

1.

Introduction
Traditional Food: A Heritage and
its Future

C. ANNE WILSON

People who take a great interest in the food history of their own region are often much less aware of the traditional cuisine that has grown up just beyond the borders of their special area. For people in the north of England, the Pennine peaks are a barrier. Crops and climate are not dissimilar on either side (even if the west can claim the higher rainfall). But local regional dishes have been developed, often based on similar types of produce, which are far from uniform and have taken on their own characteristics within the individual northern counties.

When we were planning the Third Leeds Symposium on Food History and Traditions we thought it would be interesting to consider some of these developments and the reasons for them within the Pennine counties of Lancashire, Yorkshire, and Cumberland and Westmorland (now Cumbria). Had the Symposium been longer than a one-day affair, we would have wanted to include also the northern and southern 'border' counties, Cheshire and Derbyshire to the south, and the Tees and Tyne valleys to the north-east. But because we wished to look at the traditional foods within a wider context we had to limit our area on this occasion, and to hope that a future Symposium meeting can explore the foodways of those other Pennine areas.

For centuries the oldest recipes, in northern England as elsewhere, were passed on from mother to daughter, with

changes creeping in only rarely when new ingredients or
new equipment came within the family's reach. The
method of transmission was oral, and, of course, by
practical example, as daughters first watched and then
began to help their mothers. This method continued long
in simple homes where cooking was not carried out by
servants, and is still the way in which most daughters
embark upon cookery in today's servantless homes. But
today, once we have advanced beyond the rudiments, we
have a battery of cookery books to inspire us to try out new
dishes.

During the later Middle Ages innovations in food
preparation came slowly, and for the most part affected
only the Court and the upper gentry, who followed the
example of the Court in matters of diet, and who had
professional cooks to prepare their meals for them. In
lowlier homes, a great step towards change in culinary
matters was made when women, other than the highest in
the land, were given opportunities to learn to read and
write. From that time they could record their own family
recipes in notebooks, and could also add recipes for new
dishes encountered in the homes of relatives and friends
they visited; and thus their repertoire of cookery was
widened. Daughters copied their mothers' recipes into
notebooks of their own before they left home on marriage,
and then made further additions during their years of
married life.

But another new influence was now at work, that of the
printed cookery book. Lynette Hunter has shown in our
second chapter how the printed books, even when they
came from the presses of the towns in or near the Pennine
foothills, were vehicles for the recipes of a nationwide
gentry cookery rather than of the most typical local
traditional dishes. Eventually a few of the recipes from the
printed books survived in their original form, or something
like it, for so long that they began to take on the status of
'traditional' dishes. But the recipes for some of the very

2

local and very long-established 'typical' foods of the
northern English counties did not begin to appear in print
until a fairly late date, the eighteenth or even the
nineteenth century.

Some of our evidence for the foodways of northern
England in past centuries comes not from cookery books in
fact, but from the reports of travellers from other parts of
the country who recorded the things that struck them as
noteworthy and characteristic of the area they were visiting.
Not all visitors wrote journals or diaries, and not all who
wrote journals were interested in food. Often the travellers
were clergymen, with their minds fixed upon the spiritual
life of the neighbourhood more than upon such mundane
matters as meals. Occasionally the spiritual and the
temporal became fused. A report by the Presbyterian
minister Thomas Jolly, who lived at the foot of Pendle
Hill, in his notebook of 1691, shows us the risks that
travellers in the Pennine region faced from sudden rises in
river levels following heavy rain or snow:

> Madam Lambert (from Kirkby Malham Dale) being
> with us upon a Lord's day about this time, severall of
> her nearest relations and others with them were in
> extreme peril of drowning at the same time, there
> seemed to bee a rebuke in it for their going to a feast
> at Bolton-hall upon the Lord's day (which was the
> occasion of the danger).[1]

Our third chapter surveys some of the foods encountered
by travellers and incomers over a period extending from
the days of the Roman Empire to the early nineteenth
century. The records they left supply information not only
about the types of food available and the way it was prepared
and served, but also about the reactions of the writers
when they found themselves sharing the local fare.

Methods of cookery and locally developed dishes
depended not only upon the produce, but also on the fuel

of the region, and the type of fireplace where the fuel was burned. In considering the diet of the Cumbrian counties (formerly Westmorland and Cumberland) in our fourth chapter, Peter Brears has shown how the construction of chimneys and fireplaces affected the way food was prepared. Hearthstones and brandreths were replaced first by simple wrought-iron and masonry ranges, then by the full Victorian cast-iron range with its ovens and boilers, and eventually by free-standing ranges with their own flue-pipes. His discussion of the everyday food of working folk and their families, the porridge cooked in iron pots, the clapbread of Westmorland and the bannocks of Cumberland, is followed by a culinary calendar of the foods eaten for particular occasions or celebrations in the course of the year. Several of the dishes we now think of as 'traditional' began as special food served at a meal to mark a particular annual event.

In our next chapter on 'Lancashire's heritage', Helen Pollard has taken a look at the traditional dishes of that county from a different perspective with her account of long-established local prepared foods which have survived from much earlier times, and are still obtainable today. Some of them are not very easily obtainable, and she had to seek them out in markets or in the very few shops where they can still be found. Interestingly, the markets not only held many foods belonging to long-standing traditions, but also showed the stallholders' readiness to take on recently popular foods, the traditional foods of tomorrow, in the form of joints from a chicken-on-a-spit, sold along with ready-cooked stuffing packed in bags.

Some of the Lancashire specialities are shared with the counties to the north: carlin peas and pace eggs are examples. Others, like collier's foots, Hindle Wakes and lobscouse, belong very much to Lancashire itself. In this chapter we are shown how a collier's foot is prepared, and at the end there are recipes for some Lancashire cakes.

These four chapters (2–5) are closely based on their

4

authors' 1988 Symposium papers, but the final two have been specially written for our book, and both have Yorkshire themes. Much has already been published on the diet of Yorkshire by such writers as Marie Hartley, Joan Ingilby, Margaret Slack and, more recently, by Peter Brears in his comprehensive *Traditional Food in Yorkshire* of 1987.[2] So our final chapters report the results of very recent researches into specific aspects of Yorkshire food. Jennifer Stead in chapter six has contributed a detailed account of the histories of two well known foodstuffs of the region: Yorkshire pudding and parkin. Both studies will be welcomed by food historians, and they provide some valuable insights – in the case of parkin, into its early origins in tharf cake; and in the case of Yorkshire pudding, into its relationship with other forms of batter pudding in other parts of England.

Peter Brears, in chapter seven, unfolds the tale of his discoveries about the history and context of an early nineteenth-century recipe book from Middleton Tyas in North Yorkshire. He had already tracked down a good deal of information about the family to which it belonged when he decided to pay a visit to the village of Middleton Tyas, to see if their fine house was still standing. He found it, very little altered from its former state, and the owners (incomers, not descendants) were welcoming. So he was able to see the original kitchen fittings, the game larder, the wine and beer cellars, as well as other parts of the house, and to make some drawings to illustrate his chapter. He also visited the church, and in the churchyard found the tomb of Elizabeth Healey (née Hartley), the probable owner of the cookery book.

His researches into the origins of the recipes also yielded interesting results. They proved to be decidedly old-fashioned for the period of the recipe book, but very close to some which had appeared in the printed books of 100 or 150 years earlier. Since several of them had come from various relatives of Elizabeth Hartley living not far away, a picture emerges of the gentry families of this part of Yorkshire using and refining those recipes over several generations. When cooked, the dishes turned out to be excellent in nearly every case (the syllabub was the exception: the former cooks had clearly failed to understand the role of the wine in thickening the cream). Several of the recipes, all tried and tested, are included at the end of the chapter.

So our book ends where it began, with the influence of the printed cookery books upon local cookery. The influence, as Lynette Hunter makes clear, emanated from London, with provincial cookery books reflecting London taste and spreading this to local gentry families in northern England as well as in the Home Counties. Nevertheless, some of the recipes survived long enough east and west of the Pennines to produce a lasting, traditional cuisine for those families, and they no doubt reached homes where the original printed versions had never been seen.

Together the chapters presented here provide a wide-ranging conspectus of the variety of food consumed east and west of the Pennines at various levels of society in years gone by. But they do not continue to the end of the story.

At our Leeds Symposium the liveliest discussion of the day followed Jennifer Stead's talk about the changes in the *mores* of Lancashire and Yorkshire through the period from the 1960s to the present day (not published here). The discussion centred on the growth of the heritage industry and the future of the actual culinary heritage. Already the main ingredients for some of the old dishes are becoming difficult to find. Those who do buy and cook them on a regular basis tend to be of the older generation; their children and grandchildren are quite likely either to be preparing versions of the risottos and paellas they have tried out on their holidays abroad, or else buying ready-made meals from the supermarket freezer cabinet. Less traditional food is cooked at home, and less is available for sale ready-cooked than was the case even twenty years ago.

At the same time, there is a movement towards the conscious preservation of a heritage that is slipping away. At local shows the traditional foods may be displayed on a stall with a lady in attendance who is an 'expert', able to explain to the uninitiated the history of each item, and how it should be prepared. The former everyday fare has become a subject for food history conferences (such as our Leeds Symposium of 1988 where, at the end of the day, the participants readily accepted the chance to taste real samples). The foods are thus distanced from the day-to-day life to which they used to belong. Twenty years ago tripe, sheeps' trotters and black pudding were still part of the regular diet for a sizeable section of the population. Now they are beginning to become part of the heritage industry.

The cakes and sweet confections mentioned in this book have survived rather more successfully than some of the savoury foods. Home-baking is still very common in the north of England, and family recipes have often been handed down from mothers and grandmothers. Here the influence of the heritage industry is apparent only in commercial versions – the biscuits 'made to a traditional recipe' with ingredients printed on the packet which include palm-oil (oil palms do not grow either east or west of the Pennines); the parkin in the box carrying the claim 'baking as it used to be' and also carrying the warning 'eat within three days of opening' (real parkin, if not eaten straight from the oven, needs to be kept several days until it 'comes again', as is explained in chapter six).

What is the future of the traditional foods and foodways? Will more and more so-called 'farmhouse' foods come off the factory assembly lines ('farmhouse' is an adjective much loved by advertisers wishing to create an image of wholesome traditional fare), while in the real farmhouses on either side of the Pennines the use of the freezer and the microwave oven replaces the old preserving and cooking techniques? Will the market stallholders abandon

selling the traditional foodstuffs as the older generation
dies off and demand drops below an economic level, and
will new, small, specialist shops then come into being to
sell those same foods at much higher prices to middle-class
enthusiasts for things traditional who never tasted that
type of fare in their childhood? Will the cooked dishes and
baked goods be altered, as vegetable oils are introduced in
place of the chloresterol-rich suet, lard and butter of the
old recipes, and perhaps new substitutes are found for
other ingredients, too?

The rate of change in dietary practices has speeded up
very much during the last twenty years. Some individual
traditional foods may survive for a long time yet, but most
of the traditional diets described in the chapters of this
book have already become a thing of the past.

Notes and References

1. T. Jolly, *Notebook of the Rev. Thomas Jolly* (Chetham Society, Remains, N.S. 33, 1894), p. 110.
2. P. Brears, *Traditional Food in Yorkshire* (Edinburgh, J. Donald, 1987).

2.

Printing in the Pennines: the publisher and provincial taste 1683–1920

LYNETTE HUNTER

Talking about cookery books is a bit like taking the lid off an ant-heap – the seventeenth century, which is where we begin, would have preferred the analogy of the beehive, but the interrelations are neither so orderly nor so defined. We look at a cookery book from 200 years ago and, initially at least, we read it for what we can bring from it into our modern world, surprised, perhaps, by the method of expression or the quantities of ingredients or the arbitrary-looking indexes. But beyond the book as this object in front of us lie whole worlds of experience more, or less, familiar to us. To understand why this book is here now, we need to understand something about who made it and about who used it. And there is a double dilemma since not only is very little known about provincial printing in the eighteenth and nineteenth centuries, but even less is known about the day to day domestic lives of the people who used the books.

Although printing had gone on in England since the late 1400s, until 1695 virtually all printing took place in London, Oxford and Cambridge.[1] This monopoly was a result of government joining hands with the guilds to insist on strong control over the new and powerful medium of printing.[2] York was one of the first towns outside the three to be allowed a press in 1662.[3] It was from York in 1683 or 1685, that one of the first provincial books remotely to do with cooking came: George Meriton's *The*

Praise of Yorkshire Ale. The introduction tells us that it was published shortly after a series of Bills before Parliament concerning the adulteration and measures of food; and the book itself is almost defiantly regional, bringing together Meriton's *The Praise of Yorkshire Ale*, with his rather racy *Yorkshire Dialog* and a *Clavis*, one of the first recorded dialect dictionaries, being a guide to the Yorkshire speech pronounciation. But this production was highly unusual, and little, if anything, on cookery was published in the regions until well into the eighteenth century.

In 1695 the government lifted the monopoly on printing, and presses began to proliferate throughout England. Scotland, of course, only joined the Union in 1711 and had its own separate system of printing legislation – even today the organisation of Scottish printing houses is significantly different from the organisation of those in England. To understand what happened next, we have to ask ourselves by whom the books were made and for whom. What kind of cook-books were being printed in London (since Oxford and Cambridge rarely moved into the genre)? Why not simply purchase them from there? The books, and here we are referring to the end of the seventeenth century, fall into three genres: there are the compendious books of household management, the often slim volumes of specialised cookery and confectionery for vocational or educational use, and the grand recipes from the cooks of great houses. If we move ourselves back 250–280 years to life in Leeds in the early 1700s, what would we need a cookery book for? – and indeed could we read it? Most cooking traditions of ordinary people would still have been orally transmitted, tied to traditional occasions and well-established foodstuffs and supplies. The great, and indeed several lesser houses, would have had their family manuscripts of receipts. The main group of people wanting a new printed cook-book is the newly growing urban middle classes, with more money to buy the wider range of foodstuffs that was becoming available as transportation links improved. These classes formed a group with a new ambivalent social status, which meant learning about the food of the aristocracy and using food to establish social position.

These people not only may have had the money to hire a servant but were also those who gave birth to the great age of the English housekeeper. The great names in cookery books from the eighteenth century are those of Eliza Smith, Elizabeth Moxon, Hannah Glasse, and Elizabeth Raffald. Smith was from the earlier period before the spread of printing presses, and she lived and worked in London. But Moxon was from Pontefract, Glasse from Hexham, Raffald from Manchester. Glasse went on to live and publish in London, but Moxon and Raffald remained in the north and became successful business women – something made possible only by the arrival of the printing presses in the regions and by the new copyright laws.

These days a publisher commissions a book, sends it to a printer for printing and binding, and then sends it out to booksellers to sell. An oversimplified story but in essence this is what happens. Things were different in the eighteenth century. Then, and for the preceding 200 years, book printers, distributors and sellers of standard works had a closer relationship. The people who purchased the books were supposed to get them bound themselves. The bookseller often had the book printed – after all, he or she knew what they could sell, they knew their market; indeed many booksellers were also printers. Almost by definition, before 1695, the markets or audiences being catered for were largely those in London, Oxford and Cambridge, or those people wealthy enough to visit the towns relatively frequently. At the turn into the eighteenth century there were booksellers in the northern regional towns, particularly in Newcastle, Manchester, York and Leeds, but not many, and they were certainly not in a position to influence what was published because their sales were relatively small.

1.
Title-page of
E. Moxon, *English
Housewifery*, the
tenth edition,
corrected, Leeds,
1769.

ENGLISH Housewifery.

EXEMPLIFIED
In above FOUR HUNDRED AND FIFTY

R E C E I P T S,

Giving DIRECTIONS in moſt Parts of

C O O K E R Y;

And how to prepare various SORTS of

SOOPS,	CAKES,
MADE-DISHES,	CREAMS,
PASTES,	JELLIES,
PICKLES,	MADE-WINES, &c.

With CUTS for the orderly placing the DISHES and
COURSES; alſo BILLS OF FARE for every Month in
the Year; and an alphabetical INDEX to the Whole.

A Book neceſſary for Miſtreſſes of Families, higher and lower Women
Servants, and confined to Things USEFUL, SUBSTANTIAL and
SPLENDID, and calculated for the Preſervation of HEALTH, and
upon the Meaſures of FRUGALITY, being the Reſult of thirty
Years PRACTICE and EXPERIENCE.

By ELIZABETH MOXON.

WITH AN

A P P E N D I X,

Containing upwards of Seventy RECEIPTS, of the moſt valuable
Kind, (many never before printed) communicated to the Publiſher
by ſeveral Gentlewomen in the Neighbourhood, diſtinguiſhed by
their extraordinary Skill in HOUSEWIFERY.

The TENTH EDITION, CORRECTED.

LEEDS: Printed by GRIFFITH WRIGHT;

For GEORGE COPPERTHWAITE, Bookſeller in Leeds; and ſold
by Mr. E. JOHNSON, Bookſeller in Ave-Mary-Lane, London,
and by moſt Bookſellers in Great-Britain. 1769.

The other primary mode of publishing a standard book, particularly after copyright effectively passed to authors in 1710, was by subscription, where an author would persuade between a dozen and several hundreds of people to subscribe to an edition. In this way, the book was largely paid for before it was printed, and any subsequent proceeds were income to the author. Clearly distribution was limited, influence small.

At the same time there was a flourishing trade in 'nonstandard' printed matter such as broadsides, chapbooks and ballads, which did reach the regions in quantity, as the chapman with their cottons and ribbons also distributed printed sheets along their well-beaten tracks.[4] The chapbook was aimed at an entirely different market. Its contents were popular songs, ghost stories, sensational murders, romances, wars, pornography, almanacs and such – quite similar to the tabloid press of today. A chapbook is simply a folded sheet of paper, often folded four times to make thirty-two pages. The purchaser would fold it, sew it along the spine, possibly adding a protecting cover, and cut its edges so that it became a small paperback book. Unlike the bulky and heavy standard books, chapbooks were light, cheap and easy to distribute. They were also distinctly different in taste. A good example of a regional chapbook format book is *The Praise of Yorkshire Ale* which does not appear to be competing with the serious productions of the London trade, despite the fact that it went into at least two editions.

However, Elizabeth Moxon's *English Housewifry* (1741) was making quite different claims. The format is still small and the leaves folded as in a chapbook, but there are now several folded sheets gathered together. We have a 200-page work addressing itself to 'mistresses of families, higher and lower women servants'. This enormously successful work was one of the first non-theological books printed by John Lister of Leeds.[5] Leeds got its first press in 1718 and, as with most provincial presses, its main work was to

13

produce the local newspaper, *The Leeds Mercury*.[6] Newspapers fulfilled a clear role in the regions. Then as now they acted primarily as advertising sheets for local produce and local traders.[7] Buying a press to print a paper was a sure way not to lose your investment, while at the same time provide an opportunity for encouraging a market in local printing. John White in York started the *York Courant* and went on to publish books in the same way;[8] and William Eyres of Warrington who published H. Kirkpatrick's *An Account of the Manner in which Potatoes are Cultivated and Preserved* (1796), and Thomas Slack in Newcastle printer of Mary Smith's *The Compleat Housekeeper and Professed Cook* (1772) were both newspaper publishers.

John Lister bought the *Leeds Mercury* in 1735; on his death in 1753 it was purchased by Griffith Wright. Griffith Wright, and after 1784 his son Thomas, continued to publish Moxon into the nineteenth century. What happened here is another example of the eighteenth-century printing trade practice. In 1709 parliament passed a bill vesting copyright in the author rather than the printer or bookseller and the profession of 'writer' came into being. However, apart from influential and highly successful authors such as the poet Alexander Pope, the book trade maintained an oligopoly of copyright until well into the 1770s.[9] Griffith Wright in all likelihood bought the copyright from Lister's estate when he bought the press. Elizabeth Moxon may have received very little for her work despite the fact that, as the imprints tell us, from the second edition the book was sold not only by the authoress from her home in Pontefract and by John Swale who was the most influential and respected bookseller in Leeds at the time,[10] but also by a J. Lord in Wakefield as well as in London.

Moxon's *English Housewifry* was a clear message to the London book trade that things were beginning to happen in the regions. Yet over the next thirty years, while several books did come out in the provinces, few attained the popularity of Moxon or near-contemporary Hannah Glasse who was published primarily from London. Indeed the provincial market for cookery books began to be exploited by London. John Thacker's *Art of Cookery* (1746) was brought out in parts specifically to appeal to the provincial bookseller and his or her audience.[11] Publishing in parts meant printing the book one sheet at a time, rather like a chapbook. Thacker's book presents recipes for each month of the year, and it is arranged so that each sheet of twenty-four pages has the recipes for a single month – except that the first part of the following month is printed on the last page of the preceding one. To have the recipes for a complete month you would need to buy the sheet from the previous month as well, thereby encouraging people to buy the entire set of sheets and bind them together into a book. Sold in this manner, the book would be more simple to distribute than a complete item. We need to recall that travel was still by stage-coach, lengthy and arduous, and that books are heavy objects. It would also have been more affordable to pay out a smaller sum of money each month rather than a large sum all at once. The first edition of Moxon cost five shillings to non-subscribers, although further editions were only two shillings. Hannah Glasse sold for three shillings unbound and five shillings bound; Elizabeth Raffald's work cost six shillings. These prices are high at a time when the average weekly wage for an artisan was eighteen pence.[12] Thacker may have charged as little as three or four pence for each sheet, softening the fact that the book as a whole cost three shillings or so.

However, from the 1760s provincial cookery books start to come into their own. There is evidence to show that it was at about this time that the provincial press stabilised and found confidence from the previous period of experimentation with products and markets.[13] But the growth in the cookery book market may also be due to the new enforcement of the copyright law which made writing an attractive way for women to earn money, and most of the straightforward cookery books from the north of Britain were written by women. These women, mostly house-keepers, innkeepers or teachers in the cookery trade, included among many Ann Peckham and Catharine Brooks from Leeds, Mary Smith, Ann Cook and Elizabeth Marshall from Newcastle, and Sarah Martin from Doncaster. But the most widely known is probably Elizabeth Raffald, a woman from Doncaster who had taught in Cheshire and was running a school of confectionery in Manchester by the mid-1760s. Her *Experienced English House-keeper* was first published in 1769 by J. Harrop 'for the author', and its success is attested to by an appearance of a London edition published soon after in 1771.

These two editions coming so close together allow one to make an instructive comparison between regional and London printing. The first aspect one notices is that neither is a chapbook. The book has been published as a 'respectable', long-lasting work. But apart from format and contents, there are a number of stylistic differences in design. The Manchester edition uses the older style of simply listing the contents on the title-page rather than separating them into columns with a rule. The ornaments of the Manchester edition are Jacobean in appearance, heavily ornate, and most likely date from over a century earlier in design. In contrast the London edition has lighter, geometric patterns, indicating the main fashion for neo-Classical design that had dominated the London presses from the early eighteenth century.

Yet the London edition is still printed 'for the author'. It is probable that Elizabeth Raffald retained her copyright until she died in 1781, when an R. Baldwin took it over.[14] This would have meant that she published the book herself, had a printer print it for her and engaged several booksellers to sell it. Raffald was a canny businesswoman with shares in her local newspaper in Salford where she went to run an inn during the 1770s. She also produced one of Manchester's earliest local directories which ran into many editions from 1772.[15] This is a woman who is skilled, intelligent and a substantial person of business. That she also produces a best-selling cookery book in the provinces is an important indication of the national status perception of provincial food. However, her book covers few specifically regional foodstuffs or recipes. The appearance, cost and contents of the book indicate that its intended audience is the growing urban middle class which seeks familiarity with the London tastes.

In Raffald's dedication she comments that she is aware of the 'number of books already in print upon this subject', yet her book holds up well and continues to be published well into the nineteenth century. As such it is an indication most of all of the growing maturity of the provincial presses, of the increasingly easy modes of transportation and of greater contact between London and the provinces. There is at the same time still a trade in chapbook literature, but not a large number of these books are about cookery, since, on the whole, the audience addressed by the chapbook is still part of an oral food tradition. People like E. Spencer or the Kellett sisters were being published in Newcastle by Thomas Saint, possibly the largest chapbook publisher outside London, yet their books do not get printed in that format. One of the few examples of a late eighteenth-century chapbook format is *The Young Ladies School of Arts* by Hannah Robertson, which came out of York in 1777. In many ways it is an indication of new trends, and its format may reflect its trendy status. There is no simple cookery in it although there is a section on confectionery, but it is largely made up of a collection of various pursuits suitable for a young gentlewoman including crafts, jelly-making and canary-breeding. The book is an indication not only of a new pattern of reading, but also of the changing in the roles women were expected to play in society. The great age of the competent and powerful English housekeeper does seem to have lasted a little longer in the north. The housekeeper Sarah Martin published her *The New Experienced English House-keeper* by subscription in 1795, and the subscription lists indicate an extensive pattern of relationships right across the north of England. Yet she publishes contemporaneously with Maria Eliza Rundell who wrote her book as the woman of the house, as a guide for her daughter.

Along with the changes in the social role of the audience for the earlier cook-books came a new pattern of reading which was a result of something which had been happening back in London. Throughout the second half of the eighteenth century a new development had been taking place in printing and publishing; this was the growth of the magazines. The end of the eighteenth century sees the beginning of the age of the editor in domestic books which would continue into the twentieth century, epitomised by Robert Philp and his *Enquire Within* which was drawn from the pages of the *Family Friend* magazine.[16] At first, of course, these domestic books are from London magazines and have London editors,[17] but by the early 1800s there were a few provincial magazines and, more important, there were a growing number of writers who were modelling their work on edited books: in other words individuals who were not in fact editors began to publish their work as a collection of articles. In Liverpool one finds *The Female Instructor* (1811) or Elizabeth Alcock's *The Frugal Housekeeper's Companion* (1812). Manchester follows Alcock in 1813 with *The Young Women's Companion: or Frugal Housewife*, claiming superiority because it contains no arithmetic, and Watkin Poole's *The Female's Best Friend* (1826). Newcastle produces *The Young Woman's Guide to Virtue, Economy . . .* (1817), and Sheffield gives us Priscilla Hazlehurst's *The Family Friend* (1802).

Most of these writers claim to be editors; they are not providing original work but a compendium of the best that there already is. This may partly have been to do with trying to get around copyright laws since in the great tradition of cookery writing many of these writers copied wholesale from other books, but in large the genre has to do with the length and the purpose of the books. Many of these are large books, 400 pages upwards. They are costly and clearly directed at the emerging middle-class young woman aspiring to be a lady. On the one hand, she does not need to know how to cook or housekeep although she does need to know how to direct servants to do so. On the other hand, this concept is based upon her marrying. Unmarried, she will probably have to find work as a governess, so most of the books also contain a smattering of history, geography and arithmetic suitable for a young woman. In other words the books resemble a series of magazine articles partly because of a new reading pattern but also because of their diverse function which can adapt easily to that pattern. Again, seeing one of these books we need to ask who it is for, and who made it. These weighty volumes seem to have appeared in the provinces from around 1800 to the 1830s, exactly that period when the change in social roles demanded them, and up to the time of the introduction of the railways which made distribution from London cheaper and more efficient.

A curious lacuna in provincial cookery printing occurs roughly between 1830 and 1870. It was filled partly with the products of those London editors and by the work of the great chefs: Careme, Francatelli (Queen Victoria's cook), Soyer (chef to the Reform Club, among other things), Ude and Dubois. There were also the exceptional straightforward cookery books such as Maria Rundell's *New System of Domestic Cookery* (1806) which was published continuously throughout the century, or Eliza Acton's *Modern Cookery* (1845). But all of these were printed and published almost exclusively in London. During this period the whole printing business was reorientating itself around London mainly because the distribution of books was so much easier with the coming of the trains. The provinces exhibit a considerable amount of plagiarism and pirating, from the subtlety of Mary Radcliffe's *A Modern System of Domestic Cookery* (1822) trading on the similarity in name and title with Rundell, to the overt example, but one among many, of S. W. Staveley's *The New Whole Art of Confectionery . . .* (1812–15). This work has boldly on the title-page of the second edition (1815), 'No person will be permitted to re-print this work, on CHARGE OF FELONY'. By 1821, S. W. Stavely is 'late' and the seventh edition, printed Chesterfield, carries the same warning and the same preface claiming that the author has been 'frequently solicited for many years, by several of the nobility' to write the work. Oddly enough another seventh edition is published in 1828 in Liverpool with the same warning and the same preface; and by 1834 a 'new' edition arrives from Leeds, no longer Stavely but by J. E. Thomas, lacking the warning about felony but – what cheek – with the same personal preface.

The whole muddled position on copyright was exacerbated by the fact that both Ireland and the United States did not recognise the law and produced many English-language versions of British books which often found their way back into the country.[18] Later in the century it looks as though Milner and Sowerby's reprinting throughout the 1850s and 60s of Maria Rundell's original book, was taking advantage of this muddle. Far from plagiarising, as in the Stavely case, which would only have been effective within the relatively isolated regional areas of the 1820s and 30s, Milner and Sowerby of Halifax seem to have benefitted from the vastly improved transportation systems and used their printing of Rundell to establish a second office in London.[19] But for the most part in the provinces one finds only a number of servants' books, innkeeper's guides, shopkeeper's promotions. It is not a flourishing trade, the books are resoundingly local, often in small format, chapbook-style, intended only for a small immediate audience.

It was not only the coming of the railways that changed

the book trade patterns. From 1800 to 1850 the news-papers once more led a new revolution in printing by introducing large, powerful, fast steampresses.[20] They encouraged the development of more efficient methods of typesetting and cheaper paper. Co-incident with these changes, and partly as a result of the cost and specialist expertise demanded by the new technology, came the rise of the publisher as a separate entity, separate both from printer and bookseller, acting essentially as the middle person, co-ordinating the different aspects of the trade. Outwardly this became apparent in the widespread introduction of publisher's bindings which provided the sign of the independent publisher. Incidentally they also distanced the reader one further step from the book trade by making it unnecessary to provide private binding.

The new presses meant a large initial outlay of money, in terms of tens of thousands rather than merely thousands of pounds; and yet again, the purchase was often made by a newspaper company. However, once a press had been bought, the printing itself, especially in large quantities, was relatively cheap. Because the new presses could produce material at a lower cost many of the old presses became uneconomical. The provincial trade, still running the old presses yet unable to afford the price of the new technology, became marginalised. At the same time, with the working-class uprisings of the early 1800s, the government slapped a large tax on newspapers in an effort to control them, as well as higher taxes on advertising and paper. These events put even more provincial newspapers out of business and with them went their presses. Without the new technology, provincial printers were restricted to small runs and a local audience; they also maintained the dual role of printer/publisher much longer than in London.

Also without the new technology it was difficult to break into the lucrative magazine market. Just as John Thacker's *Art of Cookery* made the most of the easy distribution and apparent cheapness of part publication, so

Phillip's *Family Friend* (1849), Dickens's *Household Words* (1852) and Beeton's *English Woman's Domestic Magazine* (1856) burst onto the scene and came to dominate publishing. The impetus for their success was partly the repeal of those 'taxes on knowledge', on newspaper, advertising and paper, and partly the standard-isation of sales outlets, particularly in W. H. Smith shops on railway platforms. But mostly it was because they addressed a new audience in an appropriate manner and at a price they could afford. The new urban artisan and middle-class woman was persuaded that she needed continual guidance in social fashion, just as she most certainly did need help with learning where to find and how to use imported foodstuffs and changing kitchen technology. But most of all, this group of readers had a little leisure time and a little money, both of which could be directed by the magazines. Mrs Beaty-Pownall of *Queen*, 'Madge' of *Truth*, 'Isobel' of *Pearson's Weekly* all followed and continued the success of the early magazines.

Impetus only returned to the provincial printing of cookery books in the second part of the nineteenth century, particularly after the Education Acts of 1867 and 1870. By this time the provincial centres, such as Manchester, Liverpool and Leeds were in their heyday of industrial wealth and the printers were able to move into the new technology. Possibly more important was the establishment of the school system which not only ensured a broad degree of literacy and made necessary the writing of textbooks to be used in school cookery classes, but also emancipated women into writing-related work. Even then the concentration of large, influential publishers in London, such as Longmans or Simpkin Marshall, seems to have meant that potentially successful books were usually submitted first to them, as is indeed the case now. The Liverpool training school of cookery's Fanny Calder published her teachers' manual with Longmans (1891). F. T. Paul, teaching domestic science also in Liverpool at

THE
ART
OF
COOKERY.

CONTAINING

Above SIX HUNDRED AND FIFTY of the
moſt approv'd RECEIPTS heretofore publiſhed, under the
following Heads, *viz*

ROASTING,	CAKES,	PICKLING
BOILING,	CHEESE-CAKES,	PRESERVING,
FRYING,	TARTS,	PASTRY,
BROILING,	PYES,	COLLERING,
BAKING,	SOOPS,	CONFCTIONARY,
FRICASEES,	MADE-WINES,	CREAMS,
PUDDINGS,	JELLIES,	RAGOOS,
CUSTARDS,	CANDYING,	BRASING, &c. &c.

ALSO, A
BILL OF FARE
For every MONTH in the YEAR.

WITH AN
ALPHABETICAL INDEX to the Whole:

BEING
A BOOK highly neceſſary for all FAMILIES,
having the GROUNDS of COOKERY fully diſplay'd therein.

By JOHN THACKER,
COOK to the Honourable and Reverend the DEAN and
CHAPTER in DURHAM.

NEWCASTLE UPON TYNE:
Printed by I. THOMPSON and COMPANY.
MDCCLVIII.

2.
Title-page of
J. Thacker, *The Art
of Cookery*,
Newcastle-upon-Tyne.
Parts issued together
as a complete volume
in 1758.

Edge Hill, also published with Longmans (1893). The famous Leeds doctor Henry Allbutt published his controversial book on contraception *The Wife's Handbook* (1886) with W. J. Ramsay. Catharine Dodd from Owens College, Manchester, published with Joseph Hughes (1897). The Leeds School Board publication *Our Dwellings Healthy* by Catherine Buckton was published in 1885 with Longmans; and twenty-five years later in 1910, Wilena Hitching from Meanwood Road Girl's School (Leeds) published *Home Management* for the Derbyshire County council with the London firm W. R. Chambers.[21]

It is helpful to have a feel for the books published in London to understand the development of provincial publishing in the cookery book area. The successful educational books just noted were nearly always published in London, since they attempted to become curriculum standards for schools nationwide.[22] Just so the great cookery book writers of the period, with names now probably forgotten – Dorothy Peel, Agnes Marshall, Mrs De Salis, Janet Marshall, Eliza Kirk, Florence Jack, Arthur Kenney-Herbert, Phyllis Browns, Rose Brown, Rose Cole, Nancy Lake and of course Charles Herman Senn – all published in London. These writers each wrote books with an average print run of 50,000–100,000; each author sold near to or more than a million copies of their books, and some, such as Senn, sold many millions. Writers of this kind rarely published in the provinces, and the exceptions such as L. Sykes's *The Olio Cookery Book* or H. Tuxford's *Cookery for the Middle Classes* indicate the rule.[23]

Tuxford began publishing with John Heywood of Manchester in 1902. Her book became so popular that as Heywood published it over the succeeding forty years he went into collaboration with a series of London publishers to ensure its success and wide distribution. Sykes also started with John Heywood in 1911, and the early editions of *The Olio Cookery Book* were printed in Preston. In an almost casebook study, her work was adapted by G. A.

Riley for teaching in Morecambe schools from the fifth edition whereupon we find Heywood's collaboration spreading from London to Dublin and Belfast. From the tenth edition it was taken up as a standard text for the Board of Education Examination in Cookery, a national examination, which encourages Heywood to include publishers in Glasgow as well. The book was reprinted frequently and from 1928 it was brought out solely by the London publisher Ernest Benn, who continued to publish it up to 1954.

What is quite clear is that from the 1870s onwards the provincial presses once more began to find substantial reasons for printing locally, and again we are looking at the question of who made the books and who used them. From 1870 to 1920, printing of cookery books in the regions became quite widespread. More people had access to print and there was a fairly large market generated in part by the London trade and its associated distributary channels and bookselling outlets. But few of the regional printing houses actually competed with London. The areas developed by publishers and printers in the north of England fall roughly into the following categories: specialist publications such as vegetarian cookery, educational text books, work by local authors, fund-raising books, company promotional material, commercial advertising and books related to the cookery trades.

The primary example of specialist publishing must be John Heywood in Manchester who published most of the works of the Vegetarian Society as well as being a major publisher of mainstream books. His edition of Helen Taylor's *Soups, Savouries, Sweets* (1897) provides a neat point of comparison with the first, non-vegetarian and London, edition of 1889. Just as with the two Moxon examples of London and Manchester printing in the mid-eighteenth century, these two editions of *Soups, Savouries, Sweets* show the relative slowness with which provincial presses adopted printing fashions. Richard Bentley's edition shows all the influence of John Lane's Bodley Head design policies and of the Arts and Crafts movement focus on design, which were soon to flower into Morris's Kelmscott Press.[24] The wide margins, the use of rules, of broad leading, of page by page design with head and foot quotations, of simplicity and lightness. In 1897 John Heywood is trying to do a similar job, but it does not work as well. He uses heavy, almost mock black letter type, highly inappropriate for a cookery book of this kind, and an intricate floral capital that is fussy rather than effective; the attempt to mimic overall page design fails dismally because he doesn't have the courage to box in the text. As a result, the horizontal rules float aimlessly creating patchy spaces of white. At the same time the attempt does indicate his awareness of the new movement, if also his newness to it.

Heywood's vegetarian publications, and the location of the Vegetarian Society in Manchester encouraged many other publishers such as Albert Broadbent into the field.[25] In nearby Liverpool, the great nineteenth-century seaport, one of the specialty publishing areas was sea cookery. Alexander Quinlan published *Cookery for Seamen* (1894) with E. E. Mann of the Liverpool Training School of Cookery, specifically for seamen. The introductory pages of the book advertise the class they ran jointly and state firmly that no more than eight students will be accepted. With the radical change brought to sea cookery over the following ten to fifteen years by the new refrigeration units, new guides for cooking on ships were needed. One of the more successful works in this field was Robert Bond's *Sea Cookery* (1907), originally published in Glasgow but later, and appropriately, in Liverpool.

Promotional books were essential if people were to learn how to use new products. Some were soon forgotten as products, such as Cottolene, a kind of margarine, or Bananine, a banana-based flour, which failed to catch the popular imagination. But Borwick's baking powder and

Goodall Backhouse products became best sellers as did the books like *Good Things Made, Said and Done* (1879) from Goodall Backhouse which ran into many editions, being printed up to 1949, or Lever Brothers 'Sunlight' year books. Promotional books were normally published in the towns where the company was based – Leeds, Port Sunlight – just as commercial books presenting the pros and cons of new sugar refineries or flour manufacturers came from the places like Liverpool where the factories operated.

More important for regional tasks were the trade related books by local food suppliers and shopkeepers. Both groups often wrote for their immediate regional audience. Hannah Young of Warrington used her cookery writing to advertise the products in her local grocery shop, although these goods could also be ordered by post; and Lillie Richmond based her work on the use of the 'Richmond' gas stove.[26] May Whyte, a confectioner, published from Birkenhead where she worked. In Scarborough the baker Robert Wells began by publishing books specifically for the trade primarily with London publishers; but as he moved toward writing for 'the amateur' as well, he shifted his publishing outlet to Scarborough itself. The format of his specifically trade related books is formal, as is the old-fashioned typography. But the later more general works are in a smaller, pocket-sized, format with attractive typographic covers. *Toffy and Sweets* (1893), *Bread Cakes Buns and Biscuits* (1905), and *Pleasant Drinks* (1909) illustrate the changes in design taking place at the turn of the century.

The most important area of provincial publishing was educational. A multitude of books was put out by and for the Local School Boards which range from pamphlets to standard works running into many editions.[27] One of the earliest is a pamphlet on Jewish cookery by Yates and Hess (1877) for the Liverpool Jewish schools, although it included a fair number of regional foods such as Lancashire cakes. Among many others, examples are Mary McNaughton's *Lessons in Practical Cookery* (1891) for elementary schools in Liverpool, the Carlisle City Education Board's *Cookery* (1907), and the *Lancashire Cookbook* (1896) which was used throughout Lancashire and went through at least twenty-four editions.

While educational books made up the mass of provincial cookery publishing, more important for an idea of regional taste are the fund-raising booklets. These booklets began to be published in the second part of the nineteenth century by women who were trying to become involved with social welfare and charity causes. Not being from a class which could simply donate money, they raised money and formed expressions of their small communities as they did so. The booklets 'in aid of . . .' became more and more numerous as the decades passed, and indeed are popular today. Hospitals, churches, societies and schools all benefitted. There is Blanche Leigh's *Souvenir Cookery Book* (1905) in aid of the Leeds Maternity Hospital, *The Goole Cookery Book* (1907), *The Grimsby Cookery Book* (1905), the *St Andrew's Cookery Book* (1908) from Derby, and dozens of other examples. Again, it was often the local newspaper office which did the printing of these booklets. They are cheap, fairly short and the contributors would all probably have expected not only to produce them free, but also to purchase several copies themselves. What are missing, and oddly so in view of the preoccupation of the late nineteenth century with regional folklore customs, are books devoted to popular regional traditions and taste although there are a few facsimile productions such as the *Arcana Fairfaxiana* (1890) of much earlier manuscripts from great houses.

Curiously, the lack of competition with London publications, which meant that all these categories of books published in the provinces were primarily for distribution there, is an indication of their firmly local basis. However, while this may have helped to record and disseminate a few local traditions at first, in the long run it could never spread them broadly enough to counteract the institutional neutralising of local flavour. By 1920 the colonising of provincial taste was well under way. Given that printed cookbooks are still not a dependable source of information about popular taste, the works from local shopkeepers and particularly from the fund-raising groups, do provide some insight into what people ate and what they were interested in passing on to other people. The books from the local education boards are Trojan horses. As the competition for the London publisher and broad acceptance into the National examination schemes shows, while some of these works may have included regional foods and traditions, there was also enormous pressure to conform to national foodstuffs and examinable ways of preparation. And as a corollary, as the books achieved national status, the cookery that was taught in schools became less regionally distinct. The process is similar to that occurring in the case of the loss of dialect in the radio and television age.

Notes and References

1. In 1695 the Licensing Act which had kept a strict control over the number of presses, and where they were located, was revoked.
2. See S. Steinberg, *Five Hundred Years of Printing* (Penguin, 1974).
3. J. Feather, *A History of British Publishing* (London, 1988) outlines the background to these developments and provides a general introduction to publishing history in Britain.
4. L. Shepherd, *Chapbooks* (Detroit, 1968).
5. E. Parr, *Early Leeds Printers, Publishers and Booksellers* (University of Leeds M.Phil thesis, 1973).
6. An account of the establishment of *The Leeds Mercury* in 1718 can be found in E. Parr (1973).
7. M. Norris, 'The structure, ownership and control of the press, 1620-1780', in *Newspaper History from the 17th Century to the Present Day*, eds. G. Boyce, J. Curran and P. Wingate (London, 1978).
8. See J. Feather, *The Provincial Book Trade in Eighteenth-Century England* (Cambridge, 1985), p. 21ff. for an account of the connection between newspapers and the provincial press.
9. During the 1760s the legal case of Donaldson vs. Millar disrupted this oligopoly, see J. Feather, *A History of British Publishing* (London, 1988), pp. 82-83.
10. E. Parr (1973).
11. J. Feather (1985), p. 36.
12. E. P. Thompson, *The Making of the English Working-Class* (Penguin, 1963/86), p. 264.

13. See J. Feather (1988), pp. 116–125.
14. Despite V. Maclean's suggestion that Raffald sold her copyright to a London publisher 1782.
15. Dictionary of National Biography, 1909, volume 16, rp 602–3.
16. See D. Attar, *Household Books Published 1800–1914* (London, 1987) for a background to Philp's work.
17. L. Stewart, *The Domestic Manual in England, 1755–1831* of Leeds MA thesis, 1986.
18. P. Gaskell, *A New Introduction to Bibliography* (Oxford, 1972), pp. 307–309.
19. At least, it is at this time that they begin to show a double imprint of Halifax and London.
20. See A. Lee 'The Structure, ownership and control of the press, 1855–1914', in *Newspaper History* (1978).
21. See the entries in D. Attar, *Household Books* (1987).
22. For an account of the growth of cookery and domestic teaching in schools, see the introduction in D. Attar, *Household Books* (1987).
23. See the entries in E. Driver, *Cookery Books Printed in Britain 1875–1914* (London, 1989) to get a sense for the enormous quantity of books being published by these writers.
24. William Morris is well-known for his role in developing the crafts related to printing and design. He was part of a broader movement in Arts and Crafts emerging from the work of the Pre-Raphaelites and John Ruskin, and eventually flowering into the Central School of Art and Design in London in the first decade of the twentieth century.
25. See the introduction to E. Driver, *Cookery Books . . .* (1989) for an account of the Vegetarian Society in the latter years of the nineteenth century.
26. See the entry in E. Driver, *Cookery Books . . .* (1989).
27. See the 'Education' index in E. Driver, *Cookery Books . . .* (1989).

Early Cookery books published in and around the Pennine region

Accrington:
Mayflower, [*Accrington Circuit Wesleyan Methodist Bazaar*] *The 'Mayflower' book*, 1910

Alnwick:
Our Own, *Our own and other people's cookery receipts*, 1910

Ashton-under-Lyne:
Stalybridge Congregational Cookery Book, *The Stalybridge congregational cookery book*, 1906

Berwick:
Taylor, E., *The lady's, housewife's and cookmaid's assistant*, 1769

Birkenhead:
Whytle, Mrs Mary, *High-class sweet making*, 1910
St Michael's, *St Michael's cookery and household book*, 1912
'Silver Queen', *The 'Silver Queen' cookery book*, 1912

Bradford:
Pope, Mary, *Novel dishes for vegetarian households*, 1893
Recipes, *Recipes from All Saints Church Bradford*, 1905
Cuff, Miss Marian Eva, *Recipes compiled by . . .* , 1908
Pesel, Louisa Frances, *Entente recipes in English, French and Flemish*, 1914

Burnley:
Crossley, Miss Margaret Ada, *Cakes: plain, rich and decorated*, 1901
Crossley, Miss Margaret Ada, *Puddings: boiled and baked*, 1902

Carlisle:
Modern, *The modern family receipt book*, 1831
Cookery, *Cookery [City of Carlisle Education Committee]*, [1907]

Darlington:
Homely Letters, *Homely letters on household things*, 1879
Cookery School, The 'cookery school', 1879

Derby:
Modern Cookery, *The modern cookery*, 1818
Modern Confectionary, *modern confectionary*, 1826
Millswood, G., *The new receipt book*, 1825
Greening, Mrs Eliza M., *Food and its preparation*, 1878
Warren, Mrs Eliza, *Cookery for an income of £200 a year*, 1887
Wiss, Thomas Carter, *The feeding of infants*, 1880
Moss, Catherine, *Every-day work in the household*, 1883
Doncaster, Mary W., *Luxurious modern cookery*, 1889
Biddle, L. F. and A. H. Elmitt, *St Andrew's cookery book*, 1908

Dewsbury:
Recipe Book, [*The Church of the Holy Innocents, Thornhill Lees*]
Recipe book, 1910

Doncaster:
Martin, Sarah, *The new experienced English-housekeeper*, 1795

Gateshead:
Wilson, Mrs Sarah P. and Miss Bella Coysh, *Tested recipes*, 1910

Goole:
Goole Cookery Book, *The Goole cookery book*, 1907

Grimsby:
Grimsby Cookery Book, *The Grimsby cookery book*, 1905

Halifax:
Young woman, *The young woman's companion or female instructer*, 1820
Rundell, M. E., *A new system of domestic cookery*, 1851
Chase, A. W., *England and America's new and useful receipt book*, 1868

Harrogate:
Eccles, Anna K., *A manual of what to eat*, 1897
Braithwaite, Alice, *Plain dinners*, 1905
Braithwaite, Alice, *Plainer fare*, 1908

Hartlepool:
Barker, Miss J., *Cookery recipes*, 1896
Barker, Miss J., *Cookery recipes*, 1898

Hexham:
Keswick, Professor and Mrs J. B., *Health promoting food*, 1895

Huddersfield:
Ritchie, Mrs, *St James' Presbyterian Church Huddersfield cookery book*, (nd)
Household Cookery Recipes, *Battersea Polytechnic/Household cookery recipes*, 1914

Hull:
Compleat, *The compleat family cook*, 1766
Moxon, Elizabeth, *English housewifry — The compleat family cook*, 1766
Pybus, William, *A manual of useful knowledge*, 1810
Pybus, William, *The family useful companion*, 1810
Pybus, William, *The ladies receipt book*, 1810
Colley, Ada, *Domestic economy for students and teachers*, 1893
Clarke, Lihan, *The 'ideal' cookery book,* 1899/1900
Milburn, Mrs Edith, *The imperial cookery book*, 1913

Kendal:
Heatherington, Mrs [*Kendal Wesleyan Circuit Bazaar*] *'The red city'*, 1909
Cowx, Miss Jane, *The Kendal penny cookery book*, 1910

Leeds:
Moxon, Elizabeth, *English housewifry*, 1741
Peckham, Ann, *The compleat English cook*, 1767
Brooks, Catherine, *The complete English cook*, 1765
Davies, John, *The innkeepers and butler's guide . . .* , 1808
Wallace, James, *The confectioner's guide*, 1826
Servant's companion, *The servant's companion*, 1833
Thomas, J. E., *The housewife's guide*, 1833
Thomas, J. E., *The new whole art of confectionary*, 1834
Goodall's, *Goodall's palatable cookery*, 1881
Good Things Made, *Good things made, said and done*, 1876
Kenney-Herbert, Arthur Robert, *Tinned foods*, 1893
McCullock, Miss, *Cookery recipes*, 1897
(Armley) — Leigh, Blanche L., *Souvenir cookery book*, 1905
Leigh, Blanche L., *Leeds household book*, 1914
Atkinson, Miss Amy and Miss Grace Holroyd, *Practical cookery*, 1900
Alfonse, Monsieur, *Homely hints on food*, 1902
Bond, Richard, *Sea cookery*, 1911

Liverpool:
Cakes Puddings and Pastry, *Cakes puddings and pastry* (nd)
New, *A new and complete book of cookery*, 1742
Garnett, Thomas, *A lecture on the preservation of health*, 1742
Female Instructor, *The female instructor*, 1811
Alcock, Elizabeth, *The frugal housekeeper's companion*, 1812
Stavely, Mrs, *The housewife's guide*, 1827
Stavely, S. W., *The new whole art of confectionary*, 1828
Servants, *The servants' companion*, 1829
Millington, S. M. T., *The servant's companion*, 1864
Aunt Sarah, *Aunt Sarah's directions for teaching economical cookery*, 1877
How, *How she managed without a servant*, 1883
Maitland, Miss Agnes Catharine, *The rudiments of cookery*, 1883
Thwaites, Isabella, *Fish cookery*, 1883
Thwaites, Isabella, *Recipes of ten days' cookery lectures*, 1887
Recipes for Use, *Recipes for use at the cookery classes established by the Board*, 1888
Thwaites, Isabella, *Further new dishes*, 1891
McNaughton, Mary, *Lessons in practical cookery*, 1891
Plain cookery, *Plain cookery and laundry-work recipes*, 1892
Quinlan, Alexander and Miss Ellen E. Mann, *Cookery for seamen*, 1894
Head, Helena, *Manual of housewifery*, 1904
Original Royal Baking Powder, *The original royal baking powder*, 1896
Dictionary, *Dictionary of 'Bill of Fare' terms*, 1897
McNaughton, Mary, *Dinners a la Francais*, 1901
Cookery recipes, *Cookery recipes*, 1910
Edwards, Mrs W. H., *Recipes worth trying*, 1912
'Silver Queen', *The 'Silver Queen' cookery book*, 1912
R., S. N., *Household guide and cookery book*, 1914

Manchester:
Smallwood, Miss M., *Miss Smallwood's goodies* (nd)
Smallwood, Miss M., *Commonsense cookery* (nd)
New Prize Cookery, *Specially selected new prize cookery* (nd)
Broadbent, Albert, *Recipes for forty vegetarian dinners* (nd)
Rex, *'Dainty dishes'* (nd)
Raffald, Elizabeth, *The experienced English house-keeper*, 1769
Alcock, Elizabeth, *The frugal housekeeper's companion*, 1812
Young Woman's, *The young woman's companion: or, frugal housewife*, 1813
Radcliffe, M., *A modern system of domestic cookery*, 1822
Poole, Watkin, *The female's best friend*, 1826
Houlston and Sons, *Houlston's housekeeper's assistant*, 1828
Vegetable, *Vegetable cookery*, 1829
Rundell, M. E., *A new system of domestic cookery*, 1848
Recipes, *Recipes, for a trial of vegetarian diet*, 1849
Vegetarian Cookery, *Vegetarian cookery*, 1852

Lewis, Miss Amelia, *A lecture on food and cooking*, 1878
Simple Cookery, *Simple cookery for the people*, c.1878/9
Buck, William Elgar, Mrs Marion Buck and H. Major, *The 'Little housewife'*, 1879
Trall, Russell Thacker and Mrs Mattie M. Jones, *The Hygeian Home cook-book*, 1883
Tarrant, Thirza, *Food reform cookery book*, 1884
Confectioner's *Confectioner's receipt book*, 1886
Kilvert's Book, *Kilvert's book of economical cookery*, 1887
Baker, Miss, *The vegetist's dietary*, 1887/8
Recipes Used, [*Manchester School Board*] *Recipes used at the classes*, 1889
Young, Mrs Hannah M., *Choice cookery*, 1890
Young, Mrs Hannah M., *The housewife's manual*, 1890
Butler, W. C., *Butler's modern practical confectioner*, 1890
Butler, W. C., *The modern cook*, 1894
Wells, R. B. D., *The best food and how to cook it*, 1893
Young, Mrs Hannah M., *The housewife's manual*, 1890
May, Mrs Ernest, *Comprehensive cookery*, 1897
Richmond, Miss Lillie, *Domestic and economical cookery recipes*, 1897
Taylor, Helen, *Soup, savouries, sweets or vegetarian dishes*, 1897
Wells, Robert, *Wells' cakes and buns*, 1897
Surridge, Miss Florence, *Domestic and economical cookery recipes*, 1898
Broadbent, Albert, *Fruits, nuts and vegetables*, 1900
Broadbent, Albert, *Science in the daily meal*, 1900
Tuxford, Miss Hester H., *Cookery book for the middle classes*, 1902
Broadbent, Albert, *Simple and healthful food*, 1903
Wells, Robert, *Bread, cakes, buns, and biscuits*, 1903-15
Broadbent, Albert, *A book about salads*, 1905
Nield, Miss Mary and Miss Annie Nield, *A condensed summary of the principles of cooking*, 1906
Schulbe, Ernest, *Advanced piping and modelling*, 1906
Book of the Banana, *The book of the banana*, 1907/8
Wells, Robert, *Pleasant drinks*, 1908
Burrows, Jessie Wharton, *What's for dinner?* 1909
Sykes, Miss L., *An olio of proved recipes*, 1911

Newcastle:
Forster, William, *A treatise on the various kinds and qualities of food*, 1738
Pauli, Simon, *A treatise on tobacco, tea, coffee and chocolate*, 1746
Douglas, C., *The summer's amusements*, 1746
Cook, Ann, *Professed cookery*, 1754
Thacker, John, *The art of cookery*, 1758
Smith, Mary, *The complete housekeeper and professed cook*, 1772
Choice, *The choice collection of cookery receipts*, 1775
Marshall, Elizabeth, *The young ladies' guide in the art of cookery*, 1777

Kellet, Susanna and Elizabeth and Mary, *A simple collection of cookery receipts*, 1780
Spencer, E., *The modern cook . . .*, 1782
Useful, *Useful hints on a variety of subjects*, 1791
Armstrong, John, *The young woman's guide to virtue, economy . . .*, 1817
Bell, Joseph, *A treatise on confectionary*, 1817
Armstrong, John, *The young woman's guide to virtue*, 1825
Arcana Fairfaxiana Manuscripta, *Arcana fairfaxiana manuscripta*, 1890
Wells, R. B. D., *The best food and how to cook it*, 1893
Keswick, Professor and Mrs J. B., *Health promoting food*, 1895
Compilation, *compilation of cottage cookery recipes*, 1899
Clarkson, G. F., *The County of Durham cookery book*, 1913

Oldham:

Lewis, Mrs Amelia, *A lecture on food and cooking*, 1878
Blyth, Harry, *Magic morsels*, 1879
Lancashire Cookery Book, *Lancashire cookery book*, 1896
Economical Confectionery Book, *The economical confectionery book*, 1897

Openshaw:

Cookery Book [*Moorside Wesleyan Methodist Bazaar*] *Cookery book*, 1907

Otley:

Housewife's Guide, *The housewife's guide*, 1838
Walker's, *Walker's new family receipt-book*, 1838
Alexander, Charles Wesley, *The housewife's friend and family help*, 1888

Port Sunlight:

Good Plain Cookery, *Good plain cookery*, 1886
Sperling, Edith, *'Sunlight' year books, 1895*, 1895
Family Advice, *The family advice book*, c.1895
Sunlight, *The 'Sunlight' almanac*, 1895
Sunlight, *The 'Sunlight' almanac*, 1896
Sunlight, *The 'Sunlight' almanac*, 1899
Sunlight, *The 'Sunlight' year-book*, 1897
Sunlight, *The 'Sunlight' year-book*, 1898

Preston:

Millington, S. M. T., *The servant's companion* (nd)
Millswood, G., *The new receipt book . . .*, 1827 & 1828
Sykes, Miss L., *An olio of proved recipes*, 1905
Clarke, Miss A., *High-class confectionery*, 1910
Gardner, Miss A. and Mrs M. Swan, *The 'Gardale' cookery book*, 1912

Rochdale:

Worrall, Joseph, *The domestic receipt book*, 1832

Salford:
A New System, *A new system of vegetable cookery*, 1821

Scarborough:
Keswick, Professor and Mrs J. B., *Health promoting food*, 1895
Wells, R. B. D., *The best food and how to cook it*, 1893

Sheffield:
Haslehurst, Priscilla, *The family friend*, 1802
A New System, *A new system of vegetable cookery*, 1821
Angwin, Miss Margaretta Carthew, *Simple hints on choice of food*, 1898
Sorby, Miss Edith, *Handbook of wholesome cookery*, 1894

Skipton:
Skipton Cookery Book, *Skipton cookery book*, 1910

Southport:
Trinity Circuit, *Trinity Circuit recipe book*, 1907

Stockton-on-Tees:
Wright, W. M., *How to spend sixpence*, 1881

Sunderland:
Cookery Book, *Cookery book comprising recipes*, 1906

Todmorden:
Worrall, Joseph, *The domestic receipt book*, 1832
Recipes, *Mankinholes Wesleyan Chapel. Recipes*, 1909

Wakefield:
Bacchus: and Cordon Bleu, *New guide for the hotel, bar, restaurant ...* 1885
Philip, Robert Kemp, *Consult me, to know how to cook ...* , 1886

Warrington:
Kirkpatrick, H., *An account of the manner in which potatoes are cultivated and preserved*, 1796
Young, Mrs Hannah M., *Domestic cookery*, 1886
Young, Mrs Hannah M., *Choice cookery*, 1888–9
Wooley, George, *The art of baking and confectionery*, 1904

York:
Pauli, Simon, *A treatise on tobacco, tea, coffee and chocolate*, 1746
Robertson, Mrs Hannah, *The young ladies school of arts*, 1777
Croft, John, *A treatise on the wives of Portugal*, 1787
Peckham, Ann, *The compleat English cook ...* , 1790
Hunter, A., *Culina famulatrix medicina*, 1804
Hunter, A., *Receipts in modern cookery*, 1820
Poole, Watkin, *The female's best friend*, 1826
Universal, *The universal family recipe book*, 1830
Advice, *Advice to a young married woman*, 1887
Sure, *A sure guide to rapid wealth*, 1875

Moss, Catherine, *Every-day work in the household*, 1882
Headdon, M. E., *Household object lessons*, 1886
Cammidge, Mrs, *Plain cookery recipes*, 1893
Colley, Ada, *Domestic economy for students and teachers*, 1893
Bell, John, *The servant's guide*, 1895
Lyttleton, Mary Kathleen, *Commonsense for housewives*, 1896
Mather, J., *Commonsense for housewives*, 1896
Plain cookery recipes, *Plain cookery recipes for use in the York Council Schools*, 1908
Grains, *Grains of gold for every household*, 1895

3.

Travellers' Fare: Food encountered by some Earlier Visitors to the Pennine Region

C. ANNE WILSON

People have been visiting the Pennine region since prehistoric times, but the earliest incomers rarely arrived on a temporary basis: they came to stay as settlers on the land. It was not until the days of the Roman empire that travellers in the modern sense of the word began to move back and forth across Britain, using the new system of roads built by the Roman army of occupation, originally for military purposes.

For a long time the Pennine uplands remained a semi-military zone, with a network of roads and forts. But local people, the Celtic Brigantes, began to live in the *vici* or settlements that grew up outside the forts to provide services needed by the army; and into the bigger *vici* were gradually introduced such adjuncts to Roman life as bath-houses, temples, and the official guest houses called *mansiones* and comprising, usually, a set of bedrooms, a small bath-house, and stabling for horses. The *mansiones* were primarily for the use of the envoys of the imperial post, though other people could often stay in them if they first obtained a permit.

The food encountered by visitors to the *mansiones* is likely to have been similar to that eaten by the soldiers and their officers. Indeed, the soldiers themselves were hardly more than visitors to the Pennine region, having been recruited in distant parts of Europe, North Africa or the Near East; after a few years they were often moved on to some other troubled part of the imperial frontier, never to return to Britain again.

A contemporary written record of some of the foodstuffs available to them has survived on two of the Vindolanda tablets, little slips of alder or birch-wood inscribed in ink with Latin writing.[1] Vindolanda, on the Stanegate behind Hadrian's Wall, had a fifteen-room *mansio* within its *vicus*. One tablet contains a daily listing of some foods written down during a week in late June round about A.D. 100; the other holds a shorter list of almost the same date, but it is written in a different hand.

The cereal mentioned on five days out of seven in the longer list is barley (perhaps, as has been suggested, because by June the year's wheat supply had already run out). Wheat was the usual breadcorn of the Roman army, and deposits of wheat have been found in forts elsewhere in the Pennine region, at Papcastle in Cumbria and at Ambleside in Westmorland.[2] Wheat has a single mention on the shorter Vindolanda list. Celtic beer, which appears four times in the daily account, was brewed locally from the malt of a primitive type of wheat called *bracis*; and *bracis* is also named on the shorter list.

It may cause some surprise that oats are neither listed on the Vindolanda tablets, nor have they been found in any quantity on earlier Roman sites in northern England. The reason is that they had probably not yet arrived. They have occasionally been found on Iron Age sites in southern England, mixed in with wheat or barley; and it is thought they entered the country in the seedcorn of settlers from the Rhineland. In the first century A.D. Pliny still regarded oats as a weed of wheat and barley, but he recorded that the German tribes grew them as a crop and lived on oatmeal porridge.[3] It is extremely probable that oats had been introduced as a crop in the colder wetter upland parts of Britain well before the arrival of the first Saxon settlers towards the end of the fourth century A.D.

On the longer Vindolanda food-list is pork fat, which

Roman soldiers in northern Europe ate as a substitute for the olive oil of the Mediterranean lands. Young pig, ham, venison and roe-deer are all on the shorter list; and large numbers of bones of both domestic and game animals have been found in forts along Hadrian's Wall and in Cumbria, Lancashire and Yorkshire, a reminder that Roman soldiers in Britain ate more fleshmeat than did their counterparts in southern Europe. Sheep, pigs and cattle would have been reared by the local people, but the soldiers themselves hunted some of the game. That at least seems to be the message of an altar dedicated to the forest god Silvanus which was found in Weardale. The inscription says that it was set up by Minicianus, the prefect in charge of a cavalry detachment called the *Ala Sebosiana* in fulfilment of a vow he had made, after he had succeeded in capturing a boar 'of outstanding fineness, which many of his predecessors had failed to bag'.[4] The plentiful river-fish of the region were doubtless caught and eaten, but are little known in the archaeological record because their bones do not survive in acid soils.

Other items on the Vindolanda lists were imported luxuries. There is a good deal of wine on the seven-day list, which must have come from the Continent. The spices on the shorter list may have been Indian or Far Eastern; while the salt could have come from salt-workings along the East coast of England and its hinterland. Oysters also reached the Pennine region, again perhaps from the East coast. Their shells have been found in forts on Hadrian's Wall, at Corbridge and at Ribchester in Lancashire. At Papcastle in Cumbria, the garrison introduced 'a delicious species of edible snail', a delicacy better known in Mediterranean lands.[5]

A number of herbs from southern Europe were first grown in Britain in Roman times, such as the garden varieties of mint, thyme, sage and sorrel, as were the aromatics of the onion family: garden leeks, garlic, onions and shallots. A traveller staying at a *mansio* in the north of

England could have looked forward to a tasty sauce to accompany his meat or fish; and the combination of locally produced foodstuffs and imported luxuries would have allowed him to enjoy an interesting and varied diet, provided a good cook was at hand to prepare his meals.

Britain's links with Rome were severed early in the fifth century, when the Imperial government could no longer spare military forces to defend this distant island from barbarian invasions. A few Saxon settlers arrived, at first welcomed as allies against the Picts; but many more of them followed, and they penetrated inland, driving the Romano-Celtic population of northern England further and further into the Pennine foothills. Thereafter, anyone who travelled through the region for peaceful purposes had to beg, buy or barter for his food and shelter, negotiating with local villagers or farmers along his route.

The Saxons were heathens, and in due course missionaries arrived to convert them. From the seventh century onwards, Christian churches and monasteries were founded; and at the monasteries there began a tradition that was to influence attitudes to travellers all through the Middle Ages and beyond. The monks offered hospitality to wayfarers as an act of Christian charity, so the traveller whose journey took him within reach of a monastery could find shelter there, and could share the monks' simple fare of bread, and pottages of cereals or peas or beans, with perhaps a little cheese or fish. Oats were now a spring-sown crop in the Pennine area, able to survive on higher and wetter land than barley. Over the centuries, dwellers in the area extended their usage of oatmeal from porridge to hearthbread, and they further refined the preparation of the oatbread or haverbread by adopting the griddlestone as a cooking implement. Monks shared in the general consumption of oatcake in the upland areas; the Durham monastery account rolls for 1352 record a *grydel pro pane*, that is a griddlestone for bread.[6] An eyewitness wrote at the beginning of the thirteenth century about the

41

monastery at Chester: 'The seats are worn by reason of the many meals given to strangers . . . there travellers to and from Ireland find rest, companionship and shelter while waiting for wind and tide'.[7]

The piety of the monks in their treatment of strangers was echoed by lay people, especially when the strangers were pilgrims. Poor pilgrims who came to Lincoln were looked after by the citizens;[8] the better-off would have been able to stay at an inn, for inns existed in the larger towns of England from at least the twelfth century onwards. York had its inns for the well-to-do traveller, and some provision was made for poor strangers through the City's guilds. Thus the Corpus Christi guild of York provided eight beds 'for poor people being strangers', with a woman to look after their needs.[9]

Outside cities and towns, the traveller often had to depend on the hospitality of private people, and in country places this was given in a spirit of charity as an accepted Christian duty. In medieval times there were few country inns, apart from those built beside the principal long-distance routes. Village ale-houses sometimes had rooms or beds to spare for strangers, and people who made regular journeys, such as drovers bringing animals to one of the great fairs, came to know which ale-houses they were, and whether there was land close by where the animals would be safe overnight. This was still the case in later centuries: John Taylor the poet who stayed at an ale-house near Tadcaster in the 1630s had as his fellow guests two drovers with thirty-five hogs, all bound for Leeds market.[10] But in many villages the ale-houses were too small to accommodate visitors, the ale being both brewed and served in the brewer's own kitchen, for brewers were often unemployed labourers or destitute widows with no other means of support. In such villages the traveller was obliged to seek a private host. This situation continued in the remoter parts of northern England long after the end of the Middle Ages.

Celia Fiennes, on her northern tour of 1697, tried to

stay at Brance Burton (Brandesburton) in the East Riding, but reported, 'Here we could get no accommodation at a Publick House, it being a sad, sore, thatched place, and only two or three sorry Alehouses, no lodgings but at ye Hall house where lived a Quaker, which were sufficient people, the rooms were good old rooms, being the Lord of the Manor's house; these were but tenants, but did entertain us kindly, made two good beds for us and also for our servants, and good bread and cheese, bacon and eggs'. Again, at Hemsworth, south of Pontefract, Celia Fiennes found the ale-houses of no help, and she and her companions stayed at the home of the local clergyman.[11]

The traveller who had reason to visit a country estate could be certain of food, and accommodation too if necessary, whether in a noble lord's great castle, or at the manor-house of a lesser gentry family. At mealtimes in such establishments there were often strangers (the usual word for any visitor in medieval and Tudor household accounts) present in the form of extra workpeople, specialised craftsmen, glaziers and suchlike, who had had to travel some distance in order to carry out a particular task on the estate. They sat in the hall with the servants, and shared their midday dinner.

In the households of important and noble families, where the lord and his lady entertained their own guests privately in the great chamber, the chamberlain or the chief steward presided at the high table in the hall, and there acted as host to visitors of middling rank. When such hospitality was offered, the food was extra good, as befitted the honour of the house. The Percy family's domestic regulations for the serving of meals at their two great Yorkshire castles, at Wressle, east of Selby, and Leconfield, north of Beverley, preserved in the famous *Northumberland Household Book* of 1512, give very specific instructions as to who was to receive particular foods. One entry states that capons were to be bought 'only for my Lord's own mess, and that the said capons shall be bought for twopence lean and fed in the poultry, and that Master Chamberlain and the Stewards be served with capons, if there be strangers sitting with them'. Again, conies, which also cost twopence a piece, were destined only 'for my Lord, and Master Chamberlain and the Stewards mess if there be strangers sitting with them'.[12]

The converse of this general and generous hospitality was that the food had to be at hand and soon prepared when the strangers arrived, sometimes unexpectedly. The burden could fall heavily on the wives of lesser gentry families, where indoor servants were few. In the diary of Lady Margaret Hoby of Hackness near Scarborough, part of the entry for 30 August 1600 runs: '. . . and both before dinner [i.e. a midday dinner] and after till almost night, I was busy providing for such strangers as came with Mr. Rhodes and his wife . . .'.[13] Thomas Fuller in his great *History of the Worthies of England* gave special praise to the gentry of Cheshire for their hospitality, 'no county keeping better houses'.

Improvements in the provision of lodging-houses for travellers in northern England were slow in coming, even after James I had delivered a Royal Proclamation in 1618 requiring all innkeepers and alehousekeepers to supply both board and lodgings. This obligation was recorded in Michael Dalton's book, *Countrey Justice*, also of 1618, in the words: 'If any common Inn-holder or Alehousekeeper will not lodge a traveller, any Constable or Justice of the Peace may compel him thereto'; and the 1630 edition of the same book added: 'that none be licensed to keep an alehouse that hath not at least one convenient lodging in their house'.[14]

The injunction that the Constable or Justice of the Peace should be called upon to settle the matter was no bad idea, for there were many people on the road in Tudor and Stuart times: pedlars, tinkers, unemployed labourers seeking work in another part of the country, returned soldiers, gypsies, vagabonds and a certain number of rogues. Sometimes ale-housekeepers themselves harboured doubtful characters: one at Acomb, near York, was brought before the manorial court in 1598, where it was ordained that he should not 'lodge any pedlars, tinkers or other vagrant persons' without permission from the local constable.[15]

But no less a problem was the inability of the many ale-housekeepers with tiny houses to provide accommodation for travellers at all. As late as January 1650, 'the Grand Jury of the North Riding made a general presentment of all the ale-housekeepers in the North Riding for refusing and being unable to entertain travellers'.[16] The constable's role of finding alternative accommodation for the visitor in these circumstances has survived to the present day, inasmuch as the police station is still the last resort for the traveller on foot who has to spend the night in a remote and isolated village.

Gradually the village ale-houses were enlarged, or were superseded by inns, so that travellers in the Pennine region could find both board and lodging without difficulty, and without having to rely on the generosity of private hosts. To find out how individual travellers fared, and what they ate and drank in the course of their travels, we have to turn to some of the journals and letters that have survived, mainly from Stuart times onwards. They were written generally by people who were fairly well-to-do, and who made their journeys either for reasons of health (the spas were very popular: that at Buxton in Derbyshire was already well-established with a guest-house adjoining the warm bath before 1572 when John Jones, a physician from the senior spa city of Bath published his essay on *The Benefit of the Auncient Bathes of Buckstones*); or because they had a particular interest in one or more of the places they would visit en route (Celia Fiennes wished to see the land at Northwich in Cheshire on which she held a mortgage, where rock salt had been discovered not many years before).[17]

In the eighteenth century some travellers took a special interest in developments in the local economy. Daniel Defoe, in 1727, described how the people of the new industrial towns of Halifax, Huddersfield, Bradford, Wakefield and Leeds received their provisions from the agricultural and pastoral counties around them, corn from Lincolnshire and Nottinghamshire and the East Riding, black cattle from the North Riding and from Lancashire, cheese from Cheshire, butter from the East and North Ridings, sheep and mutton 'from the adjacent counties every way'.[18] Towards the end of the century the romantic movement began to exert its influence, and visitors were attracted to the Pennine uplands where the scenery provided many examples of what they termed 'the sublime'. The Honourable John Byng loved waterfalls, especially those where he could stand, or even lie down, *behind* the water; he visited every major waterfall in the Yorkshire dales and Teesdale in a cold and wet summer. Carl Moritz, a German visitor, went on foot all the way from London to the cavern at Castleton in the Peak District, thereby exciting considerable local curiosity, because the walking tour had not yet become fashionable, and gentlemen were expected to travel on horseback. In 1805 Charles Fothergill made a journey to Flamborough Head, and another through the Yorkshire dales, gathering material for a book he planned to write about Yorkshire.

Innkeepers expected to produce meals for the travellers who stayed with them, but were also prepared to cook particular items of food brought in by their customers. Celia Fiennes took advantage of this system several times. She thoroughly enjoyed visiting local markets and pricing the fresh foods which were often very much cheaper in northern England than they were in London. Her visit to Ripon market in the summer of 1697 resulted in the following note:

In the market was sold then 2 good shoulders of veal, they were not very fat nor so large as our meat in London, but good meat, one for 5 pence the other for 6 pence, and a good quarter of lamb for 9 or 10 pence, and it is usual to buy a very good shoulder of veal for 9 pence, and a quarter of beef for 4 shillings; indeed it is not large oxbeef but good middling beasts; and crawfish 2 pence a dozen so we bought them; notwithstanding this plenty, some of the Inns are very dear to strangers they can impose on.

In Beverley she was able to purchase 'crabs bigger than my two hands, pence apiece, which would have cost sixpence if not a shilling in London, and they were very sweet'. And when she reached Chesterfield in Derbyshire, 'It was Saturday, which is their market day, and there was a great market, like some little fair . . . there I bought myself 2 very good fat white pullets (pullings as they call them) for 6 pence both, and I am sure they were as large and as good would have cost 18 pence if not 2 shillings apiece in London, so said all my company.'[19] The idea of visiting a local market and picking up a bargain, so dear to the heart of the modern package-tour operator, had just as much appeal three hundred years ago.

The fish bargains at Ripon and Beverley markets made an impression on Celia Fiennes (at Beverley she was also offered 'a large codfish for a shilling and good perch very cheap'); and Thomas Baskerville, who travelled to Yorkshire in the Restoration period, noted that the city of York was 'pretty well served with fish, fresh cod plenty'.[20] Further inland, the inns of the dales made constant use of the trout that abounded in the rivers there. There were few days when John Byng failed to consume at least one of these fish as he toured through the Yorkshire dales, recording his meals as well as his other experiences in his diary. There was the nine o'clock supper on 'trout just

3.
An East Riding
fisherman: frontis-
piece of
A. Mackintosh, *The
Driffield Angler,*
Gainsborough, 1806.

caught' at Wetherby; the trout for dinner at the Crown in
Knaresborough (but here his 'appetite was balk'd by the
greasy frying of the trout . . . At all times frying is a
difficult and unwholesome cookery', he wrote); and 'a
good dinner – trout and roast fowl' at Ripon. At Middleham,
'I not only ordered several trout for dinner, but now dictate
their cookery, and prevent the frying and the parsley and
the fennel and butter, and substitute boiling and anchovy
sauce'. At Bolton Castle he received 'trout, civility and
clean linen'; at Middleton in Teesdale, a dinner of roasted
fillet of beef and potatoes with potted trout, 'a dish they
invented'. At Askrigg there was a late and 'baddish dinner
of some fry'd trout and some tough mutton chops' on one

48

day, and a better dinner on another day comprising 'the trout caught yesterday in Cimmer Water and sent to me by the gentleman I there addressed, with a roasted fowl and a gooseberry pye'. His journey continued, punctuated by frequent trout dinners and trout suppers; at Settle there was even a supper which included both fresh and potted trout.[21] Charles Fothergill made an interesting observation on the trout of the dales: 'The Swaledale trout are very far inferior to the Wensleydale trout, supposed to be in consequence of the mines in the former';[22] he was referring, of course, to the lead mines.

Related to the trout was the charfish of Lake Windermere. It was sought eagerly by Celia Fiennes, but arriving in summer at the King's Arms Inn at Kendal, she learned that she would not be able to have a close view of the newly-caught charfish, for the season for taking those fish was between Michaelmas and Christmas. She had indeed already tried them at that time of year, potted up with butter and sweet spices; and Daniel Defoe confirmed that the charfish were 'a dainty . . . potted and sent far and near as presents to best friends'. But since almost all travellers made their northern tours in the summer months, the freshly-caught fish could never be produced as an immediate tourist attraction.[23]

More important than either trout or charfish for the local economy were salmon. At Lancaster Celia Fiennes saw the weirs 'where they hang their nets and catch great quantities of fish, which is near the bridge', and more weirs on the River Kent near Kendal, where the salmon were speared with leisters.[24] Daniel Defoe reported on the very good salmon in the River Derwent, and described the way the fish were transported to London from that part of North-west England: 'this is perform'd with horses, which changing often go night and day without intermission, and, as they say, very much outgo the post, so that the fish come very sweet and good to London, where the extraordinary price they yield, being often sold at two shillings

49

and sixpence to four shillings a pound, they pay very well for the carriage'.[25]

In the Yorkshire dales, Charles Fothergill recorded salmon of 20 lbs. in weight taken near West Tanfield from the River Ure. The salmon progressed still further up the river, but found the Aysgarth Falls a great barrier. After making several vain attempts to leap the falls, the exhausted fish would rest in the still water under tree roots by the river bank, and there they were speared by poachers with leisters. Much of the salmon, poached or otherwise, was sold at York and in the towns of the West Riding.

Some of it reached the larger inns, but did not always provide a happy experience for travellers. Byng was disgusted by 'a dirty bit of salmon that had been dress'd before, with two lumps of boil'd beef' served to him for dinner at the Angel at Doncaster. 'I long'd to be able to kick the landlord to whom I complain'd in vain', he wrote. 'At last I made a peevish dinner upon some cold meat.' At the King's Head at Richmond he was given stale salmon, and at the Bull's Head at Manchester, 'salmon too stale to be eaten'. The innkeepers had a big problem in balancing demand and supply with such a perishable food as salmon in the days before refrigeration. The simplest solution was to keep only pickled salmon; that was the kind offered to Byng at the Spread Eagle Inn at Settle, along with beef steak, lamb chops and a tart, and this time he did not complain.[26]

The most famous form of pickled salmon, reaching London in great quantities in the eighteenth century, was Newcastle salmon, transported in kits or tubs. Daniel Defoe therefore expected to find plentiful and cheap salmon on arriving at Newcastle, and was disappointed when there was very little, and that at the high price of five or six shillings. When he enquired about it, he found that 'this salmon, that we call Newcastle salmon, is taken as far off as the Tweed, which is three-score miles, and is brought by land on horses to Shields, where it is cur'd, pickl'd and sent to London . . . so that it ought to be call'd Berwick salmon, not Newcastle'.[27]

The seafish of the East Coast fisheries was carried inland as far as York and the West Riding towns, and was commended by several travellers. At Scarborough itself Defoe saw 'Turbets of three-quarters of a hundredweight, and yet their flesh ate exceeding fine when taken new'.[28] An unexpected story about oysters was told by Thomas Baskerville who had travelled north from Oxford. At York he found 'fresh cod plenty, but oysters in their season dear, half a crown a hundred, and are brought hither in ships from Scotland'. Like most of the visitors who were interested in their food, he was also keenly interested in its price, and in comparing costs with those at home. However, a man in Hull explained that there had been no oysters 'in the sea near the mouth of the Humber till of late, for a Scottish ship laden with oysters being there cast away, they now begin to breed there'. And, sure enough, in Hull he found oysters cheaper than the York ones, at two shillings a hundred, 'for they all begin to increase at the mouth of the Humber'.[29]

The most usual forms of fleshmeat offered to travellers at inns were roast beef, hot or cold, mutton chops, a roasted or boiled fowl. The mutton chops were very often fried in butter, the method of cooking which so enraged John Byng. Travellers tended to take both sheep and mutton for granted, but showed more interest in the large number of black cattle sold in the markets at the great cattle fairs. Some of the beasts were purchased for local consumption, especially those which reached the markets of the West Riding towns in September and October, and were the source of the winter's hung-beef – beef salted and then hung up in the smoke to preserve it; it was often almost the only meat eaten in poorer households in winter-time, and was a useful standby for other families. It was a standby for innkeepers too, especially those with small inns in remote places. At the King's Arms at Askrigg,

John Byng enjoyed a supper in mid-June of 'eggs, cold meat, hung-beef, etc., with excellent bread'.[30]

Many of the cattle brought to the fairs were sold on to be fattened up further south, in Lincolnshire, the Midlands, or the Isle of Ely, ready for the London meat market. Cattle raised in the North Riding were sold at great fairs held eight times a year at Northallerton.[31] Many more beasts were brought from Scotland by drovers; and those who took a route on the western side of the Pennines sold them at other fairs, such as the ones held at Gearstones, north of Settle, and at Long Preston. John Byng observed the fairs at both places, making a special journey to the lonely inn at 'Grierstones', as he called it. He found the moor desolate, and wrote that

> the Scotch fair held upon the heath . . . added to the horror of the curious scenery: the ground in front crowded by Scotch cattle and the drovers; and the house cramm'd by the buyers and sellers, most of whom were in plaids, fillibegs [kilts], etc. . . . My friend [Mr. Blakey, a local man], who knew the house, forced his way through the lower floor, and interred himself in the only wainscotted bedroom upstairs, where at length we procur'd some boil'd slices of stale pork, and some fried eggs, with some wretched beer and brandy – to which my hunger was not equal, and from which my delicacy revolted . . . The only custom of this hotel, or rather, hovel, is derived from the grouseshooters or from the two Scotch fairs.[32]

In total contrast was the hospitality on offer at Hawes, at the top of Wensleydale at fair-time, reported by Charles Fothergill:

> The inhabitants on this occasion are particularly hospitable; open house is kept for all friends as well

as relations visiting the fair, where a table well
covered with excellent provisions is found ready to
sit to almost any hour of the day: for this
convenience the meat is generally if not always cold,
and a large piece of roasting beef is always found as
an indispensable article at the head of the table.[33]

Grouse were plentiful on the moors around Hawes, and
Fothergill was told that red deer had been common on the
mountains of Swaledale, near Fremington and Reeth until
the middle of the eighteenth century; at that time, 'hunting
them was a fashionable amusement even amongst the
poor'.[34] The Pennine dales and the Forest of Bowland
offered plenty of game, and even when it was protected by
landowners, it was not too difficult for the outsider to
come in and do a little private hunting. Nicholas Assheton,
who lived at Downham, a few miles east of Clitheroe,
recorded several such hunting trips in his journal for
1617. The entry for 15 November runs: 'On the hill above
Walloper Well, shot two young hinds; presently comes the
keeper and broke the other deer [i.e. the second deer], had
the skin and a shoulder and 5s. 0d., and said he would take
no notice.'[35] Venison was rarely part of travellers' fare,
unless the travellers were friends of the family; Charles
Fothergill, journeying through Wensleydale, by a happy
chance arrived at the home of Mr Justice Chaytor at
Spennithorne near Middleham when the family were 'just
on the point of sitting down to an excellent Sunday dinner
of venison, other game and dainties'.[36]

Travellers' reports about bread are rather variable,
because the bread itself was so variable. In northern
England, before the nineteenth century, pure wheaten
bread was to be found only in the larger towns, in small
towns on market days, and in the homes of the gentry and
of substantial farmers. The rest of the population ate bread
baked from the grains most commonly available in their
locality: barley in Cumberland and the upland parts of

Northumberland and Durham; rye or maslin, a mixture of wheat and rye, along the east coast, on the Wolds and in the Vale of York; oatbreads in Lancashire and the Pennine dales. Inns would have tried to serve wheatbread, but sometimes the wheat was mixed with rye or other grains. Celia Fiennes objected to bread containing any rye at all, because rye disagreed with her, but was nevertheless offered such bread on several occasions, under the false assurance that it was pure wheaten bread.[37]

Even wheaten bread was not always baked in a manner to satisfy the discriminating traveller. Dr Jones of Bath wrote in 1572 about breads of various cereals, and concluded, 'But these and all others the mayne bread [wheaten bread baked in large loaves] of York excelleth, for that is of the finest flour of the wheat, well tempered, best baked, a pattern, of all the finest';[38] (see Figure 4i for a picture of the York bakers kneading it). But nearly a hundred years later, Thomas Baskerville had a very different experience, and complained: 'But that which will much disgust a south-country man when he comes to York is the bad bread he shall find there, a hungry, raw-tasted manchet, and if you call for household bread, they have none but what is made of rye, and that so coarse and black you will not care to eat any of it.'[39] Perhaps he was accustomed to manchets enriched, as those small loaves often were, with milk or eggs, and the York bakers had omitted any enrichment; or perhaps his visit followed a poor harvest, and the wheat had to be eked out with bran or pulses. Even when another hundred years had passed, Byng's judgement on the bread of the West Riding was summed up in the words: 'The bread and butter of this country are bad'.[40] By the end of the eighteenth century, although innkeepers usually produced wheaten bread for visitors, they would not or could not always serve bread of a high quality.

Oatbread was a northern speciality which Dr Jones of Bath ascribed especially to Lancashire, Cheshire, Cumber-

4.
York bakers (1)
kneading dough; (2)
taking manchets out
of the bread-oven.

land and Westmorland; but it was certainly also made on
the eastern side of the Pennines, even if it was not always
set before the visitors who passed that way. Arthur Young
in his record of his six months' tour through the North of
England, published in 1771, observed that 'much oatbread'
was consumed in and around Leeds, and was sold there by
the bakers at ten or eleven ounces for one penny.[41]

Celia Fiennes, more than seventy years before, had
travelled through Cheshire and Lancashire as far as
Garstang before she encountered it. 'I was surprised', she
wrote, 'when the cloth was laid they brought a great
basket, such as one uses to undress children with, and set
on the table, full of thin wafers as big as pancakes and dry
that they easily break into shivers, but coming to dinner
found it to be the only thing I must eat for bread; the taste
of oatbread is pleasant enough, and where its well made is
very acceptable, but for the most part it is scarce baked and
full of dry flour on the outside.' At Kendal she saw
clapbread being made, the dough clapped and driven out as
thin as paper on a round board, then transferred to a round
iron plate of like size and baked over the coals.[42]

Travelling on into Cumberland she found poor houses
built with dry-stone walls which were not plastered on the
inside, and 'a sad sort of entertainment, that sort of

clapbread and butter and cheese and a cup of beer all one can have'. The cheese did not interest her. The only cheese on the west side of the Pennines with a reputation that travellers knew about was the famous Cheshire cheese; and she had already passed through Cheshire, where she found that its large cheeses were produced by co-operative methods. It was 'the custom of the country', she wrote, 'to join their milking together of a whole village, and so make their great cheeses, and so it goes round'.[43]

Cheshire cheese was known and appreciated in southern England from Tudor times at least. But Carl Moritz, the German gentleman who walked from London to Derbyshire in 1782, was more than baffled by the way it was served to him in a small alehouse in Tideswell.

> The people here also endeavoured to accommodate
> me most magnificently, and for this purpose gave
> me some toasted cheese, which was Cheshire cheese,
> roasted and half melted at the fire. This in England,
> it seems, is reckoned good eating, but unfortunately
> for me, I could not touch a bit of it. I therefore
> invited my landlord to partake of it, and he indeed
> seemed to feast on it. As I neither drank brandy nor
> ale, he told me I lived far too sparingly for a foot
> traveller: he wondered how I had strength to walk so
> well and so far.[44]

Charles Fothergill, loyal to the Yorkshire dales, recommended Wensleydale cheese: 'the better sort of Wensleydale cheese is in my opinion the best in England, as I have tasted some in no way inferior to the celebrated cheese of Stilton'.[45] John Byng made a new cheese discovery: having had a supper at the King's Head at Richmond of 'a boil'd trout and cold beef, with an excellent cheese made in Teesdale', he rode next day along the Yorkshire side of the Tees 'to Cotherstone, where the excellent cheese is made'.[46]

Honey was another product of the uplands of northern England. Sir William Brereton of Handforth in Cheshire journeyed across the Pennines through Yorkshire and County Durham on his way to Scotland in 1635. His host near Bishop Auckland bred cattle and kept bees. 'This morning', wrote Sir William in his journal on 20 June, 'I tasted pure white honey out of last year's comb. Here bees prosper well, though it be so much north . . . In some places in this country they remove their hives in winter into their houses.'[47]

Travellers had few comments to make on the fruits and vegetables of the northern parts, other than to note how late they ripened. Thomas Baskerville from Oxford made the contrast, while he was at York, that 'cherries which with us are ripe in great plenty at midsummer, were here cried up and down the streets to sell at Lammas Fair [held upon 1 August]'. And he added, 'Their artichokes are small in respect to ours at Oxford'.[48] But he did take back from the vicarage garden at Long Preston berries of the withen or mountain ash, from which he grew seedlings at Oxford. He hoped one day to gather their berries to make the 'good liquor to drink which cleanseth the blood' that was made in North Wales from mountain ash berries.

John Byng met with gooseberry pies at some of his inns, and at the King's Arms at Askrigg was given 'radishes served up for dessert, as they serve turnips in Scotland'. The early summer of 1792 was particularly cold and wet over the Pennines, so peas were not yet available, and he commented rather wistfully on his Yorkshire tour, 'I do wish for the fruit and garden stuff of summer; but I must say', he added, 'that in general the port wine has been old and good'.[49]

Travellers were usually very happy with the liquid refreshment they found in the northern counties, and disappointments were rare. The day started with a breakfast drink, which traditionally was small ale until late in the seventeenth century. For the well-to-do it accompanied a heavy meat or fish breakfast on the lines of the ones set out in the *Northumberland Household Book*: 'half a chine of mutton or else a chine of beef boiled' on a meat day; 'two pieces of saltfish, six baconn'd herring, or a dish of sprats' on a fish day.[50] In dairying districts such as the Pennine dales, the morning drink of the farmers' families would often have been whey, milk or buttermilk. In the eighteenth century, when coffee and a light breakfast had become the fashion in the south of England, northern inns likewise offered visitors coffee with a hot roll or toast. At the King's Arms at Askrigg, John Byng had a mixture of the old and the new: 'a bowl of buttermilk which was quickly followed by coffee and a brown toast'.[51]

With the midday or early afternoon dinner and with supper, travellers drank wine or ale, and in the eighteenth century frequently ordered brandy as well. Thomas Baskerville spoke well of the wine in York: 'they have good wine in York, especially claret and sack'.[52] Although ale had once been the only drink available in small country places, by the eighteenth century the old ale-houses had developed into, or been replaced by, inns in the more substantial villages, and here tolerably good wine was usually offered even, as John Byng discovered, at those inns where the food or its cooking were unsatisfactory.

The most unexpected traveller's tale about wine was told by Celia Fiennes. She rode northwards from Penrith through Cumberland to the Scottish border. Two miles into Scotland she reached Aitchison Bank, a place so primitive that the stone house she entered had no chimney, and smoke from the fire had to escape through gaps in the walls; 'and notwithstanding the cleaning of their parlour for me', she wrote, 'I was not able to bear the room; the smell of hay was a perfume what I rather chose, to stay and see my horses eat their provender in the stable than to stand in that room: for I could not bring myself to sit down; my landlady offered me a good dish of fish and brought me butter in a lairdly dish with the clapbread, but

I could not have any stomach to eat any of the food they should order.' She purchased the fish, two fine pieces of salmon and a trout to take away with her (she had them dressed and cooked later in the day at Brampton). But the finale of her story was: 'Soe drinking without eating some of their wine, which was excellent claret which they stand conveniently for to have from France, and indeed it was the best and truest French wine I have drank this seven year, and very clear. I had the first tapping of the little vessel and it was very fine.'[53]

To us it comes as a double surprise to learn about this excellent wine in a remote hovel and to find that it was conveniently brought there from France. But before the arrival of the railways, all goods carried between London and the northern counties went by sea, apart from livestock and very perishable foodstuffs. If a comparison is made of the sea route between the Solway Firth and London and that between the Solway Firth and Bordeaux, it will be seen that the difference in terms of distance is not so great.

The ale of the northern counties had a fine reputation. Derbyshire ales were renowned in London in Queen Elizabeth's reign; and Celia Fiennes wrote of Chesterfield, 'In this town is the best ale in the kingdom, generally esteem'd'. She also had praise for the 'very strong clear ale' she was given in one of the vaults below Knaresborough Castle; and for the 'small beer four years old – not too stale, very clear good beer well brewed', which she drank in the cellars of Newby Hall, a few miles further North.[54] John Taylor, the poet, was greatly pleased with Derby ale, and also with the ales of York and Hull on the East side of the Pennines and those of Chester on the West. Hull was famed for a particularly strong ale known locally as 'Hull cheese'.[55]

The poet, in the course of his 'pennyles pilgrimage' in 1618, visited Manchester, where he was entertained at the house of one John Pinner with no fewer than nine different ales on the table at once, eight of them herbal ales flavoured variously with such herbs as hyssop, wormwood, rosemary, betony and scurvygrass.[56] Herbal ales were survivals from the days before hopped beer came to England, and in the northern counties they continued to be made in some people's homes until quite recently.

Thomas Baskerville wrote that he could not well digest the heavy, sluggish ale he was offered at York at the Talbot Inn where he stayed, so

> we went to quench our thirst to a barber's house
> where we had good China ale, 6d. a quart bottle, and
> after two or three times coming thither, for 4d.
> Here my landlord did ask us whether we would bite?
> I asking what he meant, he told me that if people
> had a mind to eat when they came to drink at his
> house, they should have cold roast beef and such like
> victuals for nothing, and indeed at one town on the
> road between Leeds and Skipton we had our dinner
> of cold meat for nothing, paying for our ale 4d. the
> bottle.[57]

Celia Fiennes met with the same custom in Leeds some thirty years later: on market day, at 'the sign of the Bush by the bridge, anybody that shall go and call for one tankard of ale and a pint of wine and pay for these only shall be set to a table to eat with two or three dishes of good meat and a dish of sweetmeats after'. She arrived on the day after market day, but still paid only for three tankards of ale, 'and what I ate and my servants was gratis'.[58]

To round off this account of travellers' fare east and west of the Pennines, here are a few memorable meals eaten by visitors to the region. The first took place on the occasion of King James I's visit to Preston in August 1607, where he enjoyed some hunting in the vicinity, and after his morning's sport on Sunday 17 August, was entertained at Hoghton Tower first with bisket, wine and jellies as light refreshment; and soon afterwards with a magnificent two course dinner (thirty dishes to the first course, twenty-seven to the second). There followed rush-bearing and piping and other diversions, and then a supper (twenty-six dishes to the first course, nineteen to the second). On Monday morning came a breakfast of thirty dishes. The king, the lords in attendance and many members of the local gentry shared in these large meals. As there is a great similarity in the selection of foods offered at each of the three, and some duplication across all three, the menu for Monday's breakfast will suffice to give an impression of the plentiful viands on offer. It was:

Pullets; Boiled capon; Shoulder of mutton; Veal roast; Boiled chickens; Rabbits roast; Shoulder of mutton roast; Chine of beef roast; Pasty of venison; Turkey roast; Pig roast; Venison roast; Ducks boiled; Pullet; Red deer pye cold; Four capons roast; Poults [young chickens] roast; Pheasant; Herons; Mutton boiled; Wild boar pye; Jiggits of mutton boiled; Jiggits of mutton burred [buttered]; Gammon of bacon; Chicken pye; Burred [buttered] capon; Dried hog's cheek; Umble pye; Tart; Made dish.[59]

By way of contrast, this is the Sunday dinner given to John Byng at the White Swan Inn at Middleham in 1792. He wrote: 'I now felt a haste for dinner, and this is a description of it: Cold ham; A boiled fowl; Yorkshire pudding; Gooseberry pye; Loyn of mutton roast; Cheese-cake. A better dinner, and better dress'd I never sat down to . . .'[60]

Next is the experience of Charles Fothergill in October 1805 in the very heart of the Pennines. He had set off to trace the River Tees to its source, and near the top of Teesdale he called at a house at Widdy Bank in search of refreshment. The mistress of the house and a shepherdess came to the door:

I was instantly invited in, and in a few minutes some of the richest milk I ever drank, butter, cheese and bread, all the house afforded was set before me with a kindness and hospitality I shall never forget, nor have I often enjoyed a meal so fully: when I'd done, I found my two females very busy near a cupboard in the corner of the room: they were mixing a glass of hot spirit and water with sugar, and presented it to me with numerous apologies for having nothing better to offer. I could not insult them by refusing, though the spirit was kept in the house in case of necessity, as a medicine.[61]

His friendly reception echoed the wider experience of hospitality in and around the Pennines already recorded by Arthur Young, who wrote in 1771: 'No set of people whatever can be more hospitable, or more desirous of obliging, than the farmers in the north of England – it is the land of hospitality.'[62]

For a final glimpse of travellers' fare in the Pennine region we turn to a visitor who brings the story to within living memory. He is Joseph Wright, compiler of the *English Dialect Dictionary* to which we are indebted for its many records of traditional food names. While still a young man, he became established in Oxford, but he often travelled back to his native Yorkshire for holidays, especially to the area around Settle. His wife wrote that before 1914 'at the Game Cock at Austwick we paid 4s 6d per day for board and lodging, which meant four enormous meals – with hot buttered teacakes for breakfast as well as for tea – served in our own sitting room'. During the 1914–18 war their diet in Oxford deteriorated – 'the bread containing maize and beans was gritty and indigestible, and nourishing foods were scarce' – but they escaped to Settle where 'in the war-time there was no shortage of meat or butter, and there were no beans in the bread.

Indeed, the bread made with its usual admixture of milk and lard was as white as ever'.

The plenty continued in the years following 1918. When the Wrights took two friends to a farm they knew near Horton in Ribblesdale without giving any warning to the farmer's wife, she was still able to put nine different sorts of bread and cakes on the table for their tea.[63] Many readers of this chapter will no doubt have experienced similar generous hospitality in the homes of northern England.

Notes and References

1. A. K. Bowman & J. D. Thomas, *Vindolanda: the Latin Writing Tablets* (Britannia monograph 4, 1983), pp. 83–96.
2. R. W. Davies, 'The Roman military diet', *Britannia* 2 (1971), p. 133 and reference.
3. H. Helbaek, 'Early crops in Southern England', *Procs. Prehistoric Society* 18 (1952), pp. 210–11; Pliny, *Historia Naturalis*, 18.44.149.
4. Davies, p. 128.
5. ibid., p. 129. Salt was won from the brine-springs (*salinae*) of Droitwich and another place, probably Nantwich, in the later Roman period, but possibly not as early as A.D. 100.
6. *Extracts from the account rolls of the Abbey of Durham* (Surtees Society, publications 99, 1898), vol. 1, p. 259.
7. H. J. Hewitt, *Mediaeval Cheshire* (Chetham Society, Remains, N.S. 88, 1929), p. 68, quoted in P. Clark, *The English Alehouse: a Social History 1200–1830* (London, 1983), p. 26. Clark adds his own comment: 'But monastic charity may have been socially selective and less generous to the poor.'
8. Clark, p. 27.
9. T. Smith *et al.* eds., *English Gilds* (Early English Text Society, O.S. 40, 1870), p. 143.
10. J. Taylor, *Part of This Summer's Travels* [1639] (His *Works*, Spencer Society, 1870, vol. 1), p. 26.
11. C. Fiennes, *Journeys*, ed. C. Morris (London, 1949), pp. 89; 95.
12. *The Regulations and Establishment of the Household of Henry Algernon Percy . . .* [also known as *The Northumberland Household Book*], new ed. (London, 1905), pp. 102–3.
13. Lady M. Hoby, *Diary*, ed. D. M. Meads (London, 1930), p. 141.
14. R. E. Bretherton, 'Country inns and alehouses', in R. Lennard, ed., *Englishmen at Rest and at Play . . . 1558–1714* (Oxford, 1931), p. 186.
15. Clark, p. 129.
16. Bretherton, p. 186.

17. Fiennes, p. 224.
18. D. Defoe, *A Tour through the Whole Island of Great Britain*, new ed. (London, 1927), vol. 2, p. 606.
19. Fiennes, pp. 83; 87; 96.
20. T. Baskerville, *Thomas Baskerville's Journeys in England, temp. Car.II.* (Portland MSS., Historic Manuscripts Commission, no. 29, vol. 2, 1893), p. 312.
21. Hon. J. Byng, *Torrington Diaries* (London, 1936), vol. 3, pp. 38–84; 96.
22. C. Fothergill, *Diary, 1805*, ed. P. Romney (Yorkshire Archaeological Society, Record series, 142, 1984), p. 149.
23. Fiennes, pp. 191–2; Defoe, p. 679.
24. Fiennes, pp. 189–91.
25. Defoe, p. 684.
26. Byng, pp. 28; 63; 116; 96.
27. Defoe, p. 660.
28. ibid., p. 650.
29. Baskerville, p. 312.
30. Byng, p. 80.
31. Defoe, p. 629.
32. Byng, pp. 88–9.
33. Fothergill, pp. 154–5.
34. ibid., p. 165.
35. N. Assheton, *Journal, 1617* (Chetham Society, Remains, 14, 1848), p. 67.
36. Fothergill, p. 120.
37. Fiennes, pp. 190–1.
38. J. Jones, *The Benefit of the Auncient Bathes of Buckstones* (London, 1572), f. 9v.
39. Baskerville, p. 310.
40. Byng, p. 96.
41. A. Young, *A Six Months Tour through the North of England*, new ed. (New York, 1967), vol. 1, p. 139.
42. Fiennes, pp. 188; 194.
43. ibid., pp. 196; 177.
44. C. Moritz, *Travels in England in 1782* (English translation 1795, reprinted London, 1924), p. 182.
45. Fothergill, p. 143.
46. Byng, pp. 68–9.
47. Sir W. Brereton, *Journal, 1635* (Surtees Society, publications 124, 1914), p. 9.
48. Baskerville, pp. 312–14.
49. Byng, pp. 78; 96.
50. *Regulations and Establishment . . . Henry Algernon Percy*, pp. 73–9.
51. Byng, pp. 37; 64; 81.
52. Baskerville, p. 312.
53. Fiennes, pp. 204–5.
54. ibid., pp. 96; 79; 84.

55. C. A. Wilson, *Food and Drink in Britain from the Stone Age to Recent Times* (London, 1973), pp. 385–6.
56. J. Taylor, *Pennyles Pilgrimage* [1618], in C. Hindley, ed. *The Old Book Collectors' Miscellany* (London, 1872), no. 10, pp. 17–18.
57. Baskerville, p. 312.
58. Fiennes, p. 220.
59. Assheton, p. 44.
60. Byng, p. 57.
61. Fothergill, p. 210.
62. Young, vol. 1, p. xx.
63. E. M. Wright, *The Life of Joseph Wright* (London, 1932), vol. 2, pp. 465–6; 626–7.

4.

Traditional Food in the Lake Counties

PETER BREARS

The north-western counties have one of the strongest yet most varied cultural identities of any English region. Their stretch of country extends from Morecambe Bay up to the Solway Firth, and from the Irish Sea across to the Yorkshire border amid the high Pennines. Its topography is full of contrast, ranging from the mountains of the Lake District to the fertile coastal plains and the verdant vale of Eden. As with its landscape, so with its people. In 1800, before transport, tourism and mass media blurred the differences, commentators were able to distinguish four major groups within the population.[1] The first occupied the area towards the Scottish border where life had been disrupted by warfare for centuries. Extremely hardy, courageous, honest and independent, they were successful horse and cattle dealers, and though very rough-mannered, were still extremely hospitable. The second group, who lived in the flatter, richer agricultural districts, enjoyed much better communication with the rest of England, and hence had acquired rather more refined manners, but at the expense of their hospitality. Within the mountain country, where the inhabitants largely followed shepherding as a way of life, their domestic habits and expectations were accordingly plain, simple and homely. In complete contrast, the miners who worked the bleak Pennine ore fields at the north-eastern edge of the region laboured hard for four days in the week just in order to enjoy the three following days in drinking, gambling, and inevitable violence.

Accompanying each geographical and social division, there would have been corresponding variations in diet, but the earlier evidence for this is now extremely difficult to trace. In the following pages just three aspects of traditional food in the Lake counties will be considered, however, those ones in which there is relative uniformity throughout the region. The first section deals with fuel and fireplaces, without which cooking would be quite impossible; the second describes how oats and barley, the staples of the local diet, were made into porridge, oatcake and bannocks, etc.; while the last proceeds through the calendar year, with all its festive meals, to give a brief introduction to the traditional life and food traditions of Cumbria. We start in the peat pits.

Peat

Throughout the Lake counties peat was by far the most common fuel, the major deposits lying in the mosses surrounding the Kent, Duddon and Eden estuaries. Some of these were worked commercially, peat from the extensive beds at Abbeytown, Kirklington, Scaleby and Rockliff Moss being regularly supplied to Carlisle for example, while those of Leven supplied the Kendal district.[2] Further inland, and especially among the fells, farmers and cottagers with turbary rights on the common lands usually cut their peats every year in the early summer. 'Flaughts' or 'topping-peats', the topmost layers rich in fibrous root material, were pared off in horizontal slices with a flaying-spade or push-plough. This tool had a broad triangular iron blade about a foot wide with one edge turned up vertically, the whole being mounted at the top of a six- or seven-foot wooden shaft fitted with a wide crosspiece so that it could be thrust forward by the motion of the loins. The next two feet of fibrous material produced grey peats for kindling; the relatively soft, moist and dense black peat below was best for burning. These were both cut or 'graved' with peat-spades or 'slanes' which had square-ended blades about

Fuel and Fireplaces

5.
These peat spades were used at: A, Hawkshead: B, Wasdale Head, near Shap: C, near Kirkby Lonsdale, to cut blocks of the deeper peat, while D and E were used to cut the topmost levels of turf near Kirkby Lonsdale and at King's Maeburn respectively.

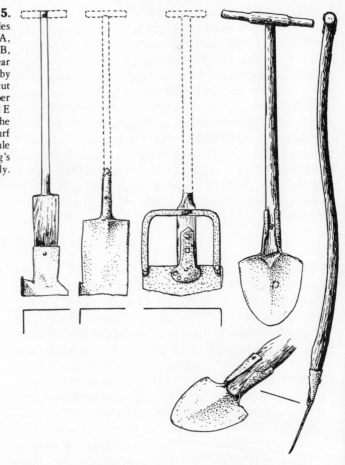

six inches wide with a square projecting wing to one side, all mounted on wooden handles similar to those of modern garden spades. Once a vertical face had been opened, the spade was pushed horizontally into the peat, cutting two sides of a long block in a single operation. The soggy peats were then barrowed to ground level where they were laid out in long 'windrows' to drain and dry. Two or three weeks later, when firm enough to handle, five or six were propped together to form 'ruckles' so that the wind could pass between them, after which they were rebuilt into tall, hollow cylindrical stacks called ricks or mounts in order that they could come to perfect dryness. In this condition they were carried back to the house in early autumn ready for the oncoming winter.[3] On the steepest fell-sides they were loaded into small hand-drawn sleds. On visiting Grange in Borrowdale in 1779 the young William Wilberforce 'saw the Tracks down which come the Sledges loaded with Turf. They are very small and in the steepest places. The sledges are without wheels and have 2 long Handles which the man takes hold of. To his heels are spikes fix'd & to the Front of the Sled against which he leans his Rump is a Cushion'.[4] Pack-horses or galloways carried the peat and turf from the mosses in 'halts', these comprising pairs of strong wicker hampers joined by a pack-saddle, in order to hang across the horse's back.[5] Carts were also used, both donkey carts and the local 'tummel cars', their bodies supported on the rotating axles of their crude, heavy clog-built wheels, squealing loudly as they shook along the rough tracks. Back in June 1800, Dorothy Wordsworth noted that Colwith 'was wild and interesting from the Peat carts and peat gatherers'.[6]

In addition to peat, the peat-pots might also produce a further source of fuel in the form of the stumps of ancient oak, fir, and beech trees. Parts of these, such as pine knots, might still retain sufficient of their original turpentine to enable them to be used as first-rate flaming torches.[7]

In the countryside surrounding the central fells, coal supplanted peat as a major fuel. Unlike peat, which anyone with turbary rights could dig simply for the trouble of labour alone, coal was relatively costly and had to be paid for. Those who could afford it considered the expense worthwhile, however, since they obtained a much superior radiant heat for cooking, in addition to the light and life of flickering flames. Numerous collieries lay on the West

6.
This barrow was used to carry peats from the diggings to firm ground where they could be stacked to dry, while the tom spade, purchased from Altham's of Penrith, was used to cut turf on the turbary of Matterdale Vicarage in 1951-5.

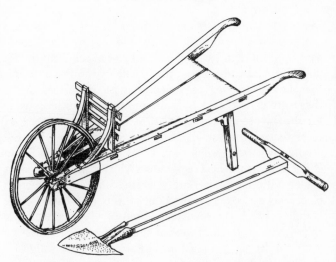

Cumbrian coalfield, the greatest at Whitehaven, Workington and Maryport exporting considerable tonnages through their ports, while smaller inland pits such as Gilcrux or Bolton between Maryport and Carlisle supplied coals throughout anything up to a twelve-mile radius. Further collieries lay on the Pennine foothills which form the north-eastern slopes of the Eden Valley. Tindale and Talkin fells served Carlisle; Renwick and Gamblesby collieries lay a little further south, followed by those of Stainmore just beyond Brough, Tan Hill, Mallerstang and Ravenstonedale above Kirkby Stephen, and Garsdale Head and Mossdale beyond Sedbergh and Dent. The collieries of Ingleton and Burton-in-Lonsdale, a few miles across the Yorkshire border from Kirkby Lonsdale, served Kendal and the south-western parts of Westmoreland, sackloads of their coals coming in on the backs of galloways.[8]

The cost of transport was a major factor in the price of coal paid by the householder. Bolton coals, for example, cost 2s 6d (12p) for a twelve-bushel cartload in the late eighteenth century, the price rising to 5s (25p) at Kirkandrews fourteen miles further off.

Charcoal

In the Furness Fells, the extensive woodland produced large quantities of charcoal both for the local iron-smelting industry and for domestic use. In 1784, for example, Ann Tyson charged Richard, William and John Wordsworth 6s 4d (33p) for a cartload of 'coals' for heating when they boarded with her while attending Hawkshead school. Its high price contrasts greatly with the 1s 6d (7½p) paid at the same time for a cart of peats.[9] Since charcoal would have required quite a different form of grate or hearth to those used for peat or coal, it is most probable that it was burned in a small portable stove or chafing dish.

Wood

Woodland throughout the region provided useful supplies of timber for the fire, the larger logs being trailed along behind the galloway, while the smaller branches were packed into halts.[10] Where bark for tanning was stripped from oak trees, the smaller peeled ends of the branches were also available for use as 'batten sticks' to mend the fire or to heat the stone-built bee-hive ovens ready for baking, with gorse, whins or furze also being used for the same purpose.[11] Dried bracken, meanwhile, made excellent fuel for heating the girdle when making oatcakes.[12]

Firelighting

To light the fire, the usual form of round tinplate tinder box was used, its steel striker sending sparks from the flint into the shallow bed of parched fragments of linen rag, where they could be gently blown to produce a flame. Alternatively a fire-piston could be used. This device worked on the principle that a gas gives off heat when compressed, a property first discovered by Professor Joseph Mollet of Lyon in 1802 (see Figure 7). It was composed of a brass barrel (A in the illustration) into which slid a steel piston (B) fitted with a tight leather washer (C) at one end and a combined brass handle and box for tinder (D) at the

71

other. By sharply driving the piston down into the cylinder, just sufficient heat was created to ignite fragments of tinder compressed with the air in the bottom of the cylinder (E), these then being carefully blown to produce the required flame.[13] In northern and eastern Cumberland the dried butter-bur *Petasites vulgaris* was often used as 'eldin', since its quick burning ignited the major fuel. 'Bullens', 'bunnels' or 'spoots', the dried stems of kesh or cow-parsnip, were used for similar purposes, the Reverend Hutton of Beetham recording how 'a ruddy cheeked lad threw on a bullen to make a 'loww' [or blaze] for its mother to find her loup'.[14] Fire-lighting was a particularly rare occurrence in many households, however, especially in peat burning areas where, by careful management, the fire could continue to burn for centuries at a time. John Briggs left a remarkably detailed account of lighting a peat fire in the early nineteenth century in his *Letters from the Lakes*. At the centre of the open hearth at the inn at Kentmere, his 'Venus of a waiting maid erected a fire. This seemed to be a feat of skill; for first she collected all the red fragments of the former fire and placed them in a neat heap. Then she surrounded this heap of fire with a circle of half peats, set on end; and again with two rows of half peats set on end. The hollow in the middle was then filled with small fragments of peat, so as to raise highest in the middle. In about five minutes the fire began to burn brightly . . .'

Fireplaces

Writing in 1847, John Gough recorded how the older houses in this region were of timber A-framed crucks clad with stone walls and thatched roofs, the floor of the central common hall or kitchen being coarsely paved with pebbles or simply lined with beaten loam.[15] It was not furnished with a fire grate, but the fuel and ashes were laid in a heap upon the hearth. The chimney was three or four yards in diameter, and continued open at the front to the height of a man; in its capacious funnel various joints of beef,

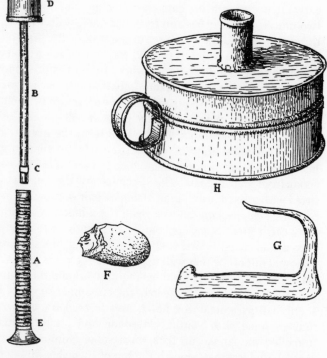

7.
To make fire, tinder was ignited either in the fire-piston (comprising a brass barrel A, steel piston B, leather washer C, tinder container D, and removable end E), or with sparks struck from flint F and steel G in a tinder-box H such as this example from Hawkshead.

mutton and pork hung to dry in the smoke which rose above the heads of the family as they sat around the fire. Over the middle of the hearth appeared a long sooty chain descending from a cross-beam or rannel-balk, and ending in a crook which was strong enough to bear the heaviest kettles then in use. This description suggests that the earliest clay and wattle-lined chimneys were circular in plan, a very convenient arrangement which would enable everyone to sit around the fire, just as earlier peoples had sat around camp-fires or central hearths for countless centuries. 'Roundabout' hearths of this kind were also common in parts of County Antrim almost within living memory.[16]

The earliest surviving hearths of late seventeenth and early eighteenth century date are all rectangular in plan. In two-unit houses they back on to an end-gable wall, while in three-unit houses they back on to the wall of the 'hallan', the cross-passage which separated the houseplace with its fireplace from the down-house where fuel was stored and brewing and baking undertaken. In both locations, anyone looking towards the fireplace would see a passage or 'mell' leading to a door at one end of the gable or hallan wall.[17] A screen or heck separated this passage from the hearth, a vertical heck-post running up its front edge to support a heavy cross-beam or bressumer which ran across the whole room from wall to wall. The inner face of the heck was fitted with a fixed bench seat, a single chair occupying the opposite side, backing on to a small fire window which lit the hearth area. Spice-cupboards, frequently with finely carved and dated doors, and other 'keeping holes' were hollowed out of the rear wall to provide convenient storage places for all those small things required around the main cooking place. Above the hearth, the bressumer supported a tall half-pyramidal fire-hood, constructed of vertical timbers lined with wattle, clay daub and plaster. This funnelled the smoke up to a short stone chimney stack cantilevered out just beneath the top of the gable. In later examples, the fire-hood was built entirely of stone, its outline having a graceful ogee shape in contrast to the straight sides of its timber-framed forbears. Frequently the heavy Lake District rains trickled down the inside of these chimneys, mingling with the soot to form a black unctuous liquor called hallen-drop which then fell on to the heads of those trying to keep warm around the fire below.

On the hearthstones, usually laid a few inches higher than the floor, the earliest fires were laid as a single heap of smouldering peat. Hearth furniture in the form of iron firedogs might also be used to retain logs when timber was being burned, while for coal a raised iron firebasket was mounted between a pair of low masonry hobs. For cooking,

8.
This sectional sketch based on High Birk House in Little Langdale shows a typical seventeenth–eighteenth-century hearth arrangement. The door, right, leads into the mell or short entrance passage which is separated from the hearth itself by a vertical masonry heck or screen. The fireplace, oven, and boiler are all nineteenth century insertions into what was originally an open area equipped with the spice cupboard in the rear wall and illuminated by the fire window to the left. In the bedroom above, the smoke from the hearth is conducted up the pyramid-shaped timber-framed smoke-hood into the cantilevered stone chimney-stack, and eventually out through a characteristic round Lake District chimney.

the pots were either suspended by a chain from the rannel-balk above, or stood on a short three-legged iron stand called a brandreth placed in the middle of the fire. Around 1800 the Reverend Hutton visited a young widow near Beetham, finding her 'sat on a three-legged stool, and a dim coal smoked within the rim of a brandreth, over which a sooty reckoncrook hung dangling from a black randletree. The walls were plastered with dirt, and a ladder with hardly a rung, was reared into a loft'.[18]

Probably in the mid to late eighteenth century these great open fireplaces were made much more convenient and comfortable by ceiling each end of the chimney opening at bressumer level, so that people could sit by the fire without any risk of falling soot, hallen drop or other conspicuous dirt. The narrowed chimney was then contained within shallow side-walls extending upwards from the hearth to a fire-hood of stone or timber. Frequently a swinging fire-crane equipped with a number of ratten-hooks or adjustable iron pot-hangers was added at the same time so that hanging pots, kettles and girdles could be hung over the fire as necessary.

By the late eighteenth century at least, these large chimney openings were being ceiled across entirely, the fireplace now standing within a masonry chimney stack which extended up to roof level in the modern manner, entirely replacing the old timber-framed fire hood. In addition to enabling iron grates and ranges of the most up-to-date design to be installed, this improvement also provided much more space in the bedroom above. All fireplaces built after this date followed exactly the same pattern.

Up to around 1800 the simple wrought-iron range made in the form of a raised horizontal-barred firebasket mounted between two low masonry hobs satisfied the needs of almost every household, but from that time cast iron ranges began to be introduced, most of them originating from the small foundries which sprang up in all the major market towns. By the middle and late Victorian period, however, the local ironmongers were able to use the

9.
(top) This cottage fireplace, drawn by W. Collingwood in Ambleside in 1841, has its peat fire burning on the hearth between stone hobs, the smoke-hood above being fitted with a swinging chimney-crane.
(bottom) Painted by Emily Nicholson in the 1850s, this hearth has a stone bench built against the heck (right) while the fire itself burns within a wrought-iron basket fitted above a sunken ashpit.

developing railway system to supply ranges made by quite distant manufacturers. Around the 1860s, for example, Matthew Redhead of Kendal stocked the catalogues of the following companies:

Cockey & Macfarlane	Glasgow
Elmbank Foundry & Smithfield Iron Works, 1868–9	,,
Ritchie, Watson & Co., Etna Foundry	,,
Thos. Allan & Sons, Springbank Ironworks, 1871	,,
McDowell, Steven & Co., Milton Ironworks, 1868	,,
Carron Ironworks, 1870	Falkirk
Falkirk Ironworks, 1863–7–8	,,
Wm. Bennet Jnr.	Liverpool
W.I.F.R. (Yorkshire Ranges)	South Yorkshire
Wm. Owen, Weathill Foundry, 1867	Rotherham
Picksley, Sims & Co., Bedford Foundry, 1855	Leigh

The simplest ranges were little more than cast-iron versions of the old wrought-iron examples, their horizontal firebars being arranged between two moulded iron plates which re-faced the fronts of the former masonry hobs. One elaboration on this basic form was the provision of a back- or side-boiler, which was filled from a flap in the top of the hob, the hot water then being drawn off through a brass tap mounted on one of the faceplates. In addition, a hot-air oven could be constructed in the recess between the chimney breast and the side walls of the hearth area. Founders such as Joseph Bowerbank of Penrith could supply these in sizes from 15" x 20" overall for small cottages to 36" x 40" for large houses, each being supplied with an appropriate grate-back, soot-scrapers to clean the flues around the oven, and a damper to control the heat. An oven of this type, made the whole operation of baking much simpler, quicker, and cleaner, avoiding all the troublesome smoke, ash, and temperature problems of the old stone beehive ovens.

The ideal range or 'kitchener' incorporated boiler, hot-air oven, open fire and chimney crane in one well-designed

10.
Also painted by Emily Nicholson around 1850, this fireplace in the Eden Valley has its fire burning in a wrought-iron basket standing between two stone hobs.

comprehensive unit, which fitted snugly within the jambs of the fireplace. These became increasingly popular from the 1820s and 30s, similar models still being installed up to a century later. Their individual designs might vary

79

11.
Both of these traditional open hearths have had their original smoke-hoods replaced by masonry chimney-stacks probably in the late eighteenth to early nineteenth centuries. The range at Low Hollins Farm in the Vale of Lorton (top) has a boiler in its left-hand hob, and a hot-air oven in its right-hand recess. That at Brotherikeld in upper Eskdale (bottom) has a typical mid-nineteenth century design, incorporating a hot-air oven and a swinging chimney crane.

greatly with regard to their decorative detailing etc., but in broad terms they were all very similar. The fire grate occupied the centre of the range, with the hot-air oven mounted on a hob at one side, and a hob, perhaps incorporating a boiler on the other. To control the smoke, 'coves' made either of slabs of stone or sheets of moulded iron arched across the area above the hob and fire grate, still leaving sufficient space here for a chimney crane with its ratten crooks.

At the end of the nineteenth century a number of local foundries began to produce 'Anglo-American Cooking Ranges', adopting 'the American style of Range to our British fireplaces'. Instead of being built-in, these ranges were designed as a rectangular box incorporating a closed firebox, an oven, boiler, and a number of boiling rings, the whole arrangement standing on four strong feet, and having a cast-iron flue-pipe to carry off the smoke. Marketed under local names such as 'The Skiddaw' or 'The Pennine', they proved both versatile and extremely economical, consuming less than half the fuel required by the traditional open range. Their success probably paved the way for improved forms of insulated closed stoves, including the renowned 'Aga' still so popular today.

Girdles and backstones

The traditional utensil for baking oatcakes was the girdle, a flat iron plate perhaps 26 inches (66 cm) in diameter having two small looped handles at the sides by which its position could be adjusted, and by which it could be hung against the wall when not in use. It was heated by being placed flat on top of a brandreth, a short tripod stand made of iron which was planted amid the fire burning on the hearth stone. For use on the later hearths and ranges which were provided with a chimney crane, the girdles were made with a vertical bow handle, a swivel ring mounted at its apex enabling it to be hung over the fire from a ratten-crook.

Larger versions of the girdle called backstones were built into the domestic rooms of many of the larger farmhouses. Standing to table-height in a convenient corner, the horizontal top was formed by two large flat iron sheets about 30 inches (76 cm) square. These were

12.
From the late eighteenth century, most fireplaces were built in the usual modern form, their square-headed lintelled openings being housed in vertical masonry chimney stacks. Both of these examples, painted by Emily Nicholson *c.* 1850 (top) and drawn by W. Collingwood in Ambleside on August 16th, 1841 (bottom) have iron firebaskets set between masonry hobs.

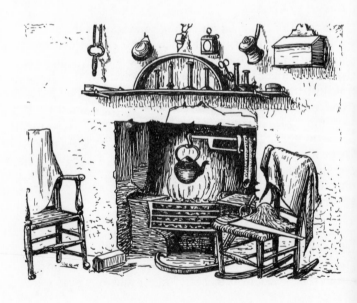

13.
Most of the small foundries set up in the major market towns in the early nineteenth century produced their own variety of kitchener or kitchen range. This particular example was manufactured as the 'Hot-air Oven Cottage Range, No. B7' by Joseph Bowerbank of Penrith, who sold them for £4 to £4.67 each.

Directions and a rough Plan are here given by which any intelligent Mason may fix them.

PLAN FOR SETTING HOT-AIR OVENS

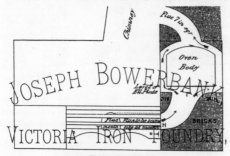

(FRONT ELEVATION)
NO FLUE REQUIRED AT THE END OF OVEN BODY.

View of Section showing Flue on a level with top of front and ell plate at T, and on a level with Grate bottom at H.

JOSEPH BOWERBANK, Victoria Iron Foundry, PENRITH.

14.

The late nineteenth century saw the introduction of American-style portable closed stoves made of cast iron, such as this 'Anglo-American Cooking Range' produced at Joseph Bowerbank's Penrith Foundry.

ANGLO-AMERICAN COOKING RANGES.

I have much pleasure in drawing attention to the new "ANGLO-AMERICAN" COOKING RANGES, which are admitted to be the most perfect yet introduced. They are constructed to meet a want long felt, viz.—to adopt the American style of Range to our British fireplaces. After many experiments I have produced these Ranges, which are complete in their arrangements for all kinds of Cooking, and are most perfect in operation. These Ranges will do double the amount of work of any close Range at their price, and with only one-half, or, even under the most unfavourable circumstances, two-thirds the amount of fuel.

As savers of Coal and Labour they are unequalled.

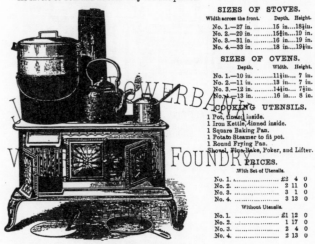

SIZES OF STOVES.

Width across the front.	Depth.	Height.
No. 1.—27 in.	15 in.	18½ in.
No. 2.—29 in.	15¾ in.	19 in.
No. 3.—31 in.	16 in.	19 in.
No. 4.—33 in.	18 in.	19½ in.

SIZES OF OVENS.

	Depth.	Width.	Height.
No. 1.	10 in.	11½ in.	7 in.
No. 2.	11 in.	13 in.	7 in.
No. 3.	12 in.	14½ in.	7½ in.
No. 4.	13 in.	16 in.	8 in.

COOKING UTENSILS.

1 Pot, tinned inside.
1 Iron Kettle, tinned inside.
1 Square Baking Pan.
1 Potato Steamer to fit pot.
1 Round Frying Pan.
Shovel, Flue Rake, Poker, and Lifter.

PRICES.

With Set of Utensils.

	£	s	d
No. 1.	£2	4	0
No. 2.	2	11	0
No. 3.	3	1	0
No. 4.	3	13	0

Without Utensils.

	£	s	d
No. 1.	£1	12	0
No. 2.	1	17	0
No. 3.	2	4	0
No. 4.	2	13	0

"THE SKIDDAW."

FOUR SIZES, Nos. 1, 2, 3, & 4.

This is a most desirable Range for small Families. It is so arranged that it may be set back between the jambs. It has accommodation on top for three Pots; also a good sized Oven with entrance from the front.

heated by a fireplace below, the vertical freestone slab forming the front of the backstone having suitable holes pierced in it for the insertion of fuel and the extraction of the ash. The fuel varied from place to place, furze or bracken being used extensively, while at Lupton local people used chips of wood from Gatebeck gunpowder factory.[20] These large backstones were utilised to make oatcakes in

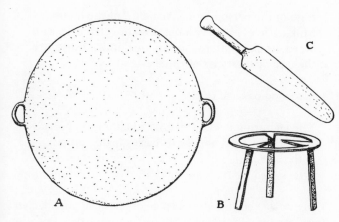

15.
The traditional oatcake of the Lake Counties, clapbread, was baked on an iron girdle (A, this example being 26 ins. in diameter) mounted over a peat fire on a brandreth (B). The spurtle (C) was used to turn oatcakes at Ulcatrow, Matterdale.

very large batches; a number of women earned their living by travelling from one house to another to do the baking. One lady from Bootle in Cumberland charged 1/6 (7½p) and a glass of gin each day for this service around 1900, perhaps baking up to twenty stones of meal at a single session.[21]

The traditional diet of the working population of the Lake counties during the late eighteenth century is concisely described in the two following passages. The first is from northern Cumberland, and the second from Westmorland:

Traditional diet

The common diet is homely, but wholesome fare, and rather peculiar to this county. Bread is made of barley, or barley and rye, which is generally leavened, and baked in large loaves; but towards the borders of Scotland, unleavaned cakes, locally called *scons* prevail. *Hasty-pudding*, or thick pottage, is a dish which almost universally forms the breakfast, and often the supper: it is made of oatmeal boiled with water to a thick pulp, and is eaten along with a little butter, milk, treacle, or beer, according to the

taste of the person, or convenience of the family.
Milk, either boiled with oatmeal, or eaten cold with
bread; as also butter, and skimmed milk cheese, are
the principal articles of Cumberland food.[22]

The second passage runs:

> The labouring poor . . . subsisted chiefly on porridge
> made of oat-meal or dressed barley boiled in milk,
> with the addition of oat bread, butter, onions, and a
> little salted meat occasionally.[23]

Thus we can see the dependence on oatmeal porridge and
dairy produce throughout the region, and the transition
from leavened barley or maslin bread in the north to flat
oatcakes in the south. As one writer has recorded:

> then they lived mainly on poddish and taties.
> Poddish was t'foundation stean, and if they're well
> made there's nowt to lick 'em yet; they act like a
> poultice on your stomach, and they make bone as
> well as brain. [During the Napoleonic wars]
> everything in the way o' bread stuff down to t' very
> salt was both terrible scarce and parlous dear. I've
> often heard my mother say that when she was
> making us bairns our poddish that she didn't know
> sometimes whether to leave out t' meal or t' salt.
> Around Coniston and Kirkby t' poor folks were
> fairly hungered out, so that they had to go into t'
> dyke sides and gather nettles to make nettle poddish
> on. All was fish that came to t' net with them, for
> they picked up herbs of all kinds to boil in it.[24]

The importance of oatmeal as the basic staff of life in this
region was clearly recognised in the form of relief given to
the poor, especially when on the road. The elderly sailor
whom the Wordsworths met near Rydal was easily

recognised as a beggar by 'His bags [which] hung over each shoulder and lay on each side of him, below his breast. One was brownish and of coarse stuff, the other was white with meal on the outside, and his blue waistcoat was whitened with meal' which he had begged or 'lated' along the road. If he could persuade someone to give him access to a pot and a fire, this meal would soon provide him with a sustaining dish of porridge.[25]

Porridge

The porridge was slowly cooked in an iron pot hanging over the fire, its thick contents being stirred with a wooden thyvel, poddish stock or keall stick to prevent it burning or forming into hard lumps. When ready, it was poured into a bowl suitable to the size of the family, and placed in the centre of the table. 'Everyone then sat around and dipped their wooden spoons or "gobsticks" into the fragrant mess, each bringing out a portion, and again bringing the charged spoon into a basin or tin of skim-milk, conveying the relished contents to the mouth and often with considerable dispatch.'[26] In central and northern Cumberland the milk was served in 'bickers', these being small cooper-made tubs from which one stave rose vertically to provide a strong and convenient handle: 'The porridge was ready, and Mercy set the wooden bowl on the table. "I's fullen thy bicker, my lass", said Gubblum'.[28]

Other moist oatmeal dishes eaten around this period included 'drammock', a simple east Cumbrian mixture of oatmeal and water, and the more widespread 'crowdy' for which the oatmeal was mixed either with broth in which beef was boiling, or with the marrow of beef or mutton bones to make a very quick and convenient hot savoury meal. Fine oatmeal could also be made into sowens by being steeped in cold water overnight. The mixture was then strained through a fine sieve, the residue being squeezed in the hands to extract every drop of liquor. This liquor was then boiled, and continuously stirred until it thickened, and was ready to be poured into bowls freshly rinsed with cold water, and left in a cool place to set. 'There's lots of maks o' sowins but they're no yan better ner anudder. Soor sowins, sweet sowins, hef sowins, cauld sowins, and its "Oh, fer Westmerlan' sowins an' cream".' Other accompaniments to this cool, slightly sharp oatmeal jelly might include honey, milk, ale or wine, although the latter would never appear on the farm-worker's supper table, where sowens formed a regular dish.[29]

Clapbread

The method of making another major oatmeal food, clapbread, was first described in detail by the diarist Celia Fiennes in 1698:

> . . . they mix their flour with water so soft as to
> rowle it in their hands into a ball, and then they
> have a board made round and something hollow in
> the middle rising by degrees all round to the edge a
> little higher but so little as one would take it to be
> only a board warp'd, this is to cast out the cake thinn
> and so they clap it round and drive it to the edge in a
> due proportion till drove as thinn as a paper, and
> still they clap it and drive it round, and they have a
> plaite of iron same size with their clap board and so
> shove off the cake on it and so set it on coales and
> bake it . . . if their iron plaite is smooth and they
> take care their coals or embers are not too hot but
> just to make it look yellow it will bake and be as
> crisp and pleasant to eate as any thing you can
> imagine.[30]

In the 1820s, the same method was still being used, with the housewife 'sat down on the floor, with the back-board on her knees. On this board she laid a piece of paste, which she clapped or beat with her hand, till it expanded to a broad, thin cake – hence the name of clapbread'.[31] From

around this date however, the clapping technique appears
to have been largely replaced by rolling, as in the following
account of 1794:

> The bread generally eaten in the county is made
> from oatmeal. Water and oatmeal are kneaded
> together into a paste without any leaven; this paste
> is rolled into a circular cake of about twenty inches
> in diameter, and is placed upon a thin flat plate of
> iron, called a girdle, under which a fire is put, and
> the cake thus baked goes by the name of clap-bread,
> and is to be seen at almost every table in the county.
> The meal is mostly ground to such a degree of
> fineness, that a measure of sixteen quarts will weigh
> sixteen pounds. Farmers, labourers, and
> manufacturers, usually have fifteen cakes made from
> sixteen pounds of meal, and as many baked in a day
> as will serve their families for a month. Such of the
> gentry as eat this sort of bread, most of them now
> eating bread made from wheat, have it baked much
> more frequently, and also much thinner. A
> labouring man will eat sixteen pounds of meal made
> into bread in a fortnight: the price of sixteen pounds
> of meal is variable from 1s. 6d. to 2s. 6d.; the
> medium is 2s. which gives 1s. a week for each
> labourer for bread.[32]

In the 1940s, Dr Henry Bedford was still able to record
how the clapcake or havercake of this region was made by
interviewing those who either made it themselves, or
remembered how others had made it.[33] The methods were
all remarkably similar, fine oatmeal first being worked into
a soft dough with warm water, before being kneaded
thoroughly and rolled out into a large cake, up to almost a
yard diameter and about as thin as an old sixpence (c.
1/16" or 2 mm), dry oats being sprinkled above and below
it to prevent it from sticking. Very skilled makers could

turn the cake by tossing it on the board like a pancake, while others would turn it and transfer it on to the girdle by rolling it on and off the rolling pin. Once on the girdle, all surplus meal was brushed away with a goose feather. Here it cooked until the edges began to curl, when it was turned over to cook on the other side. To dry off, the cake was next propped up on a cake stool or havercake maiden, a small wooden easel, placed in front of the open fire. Ling had the best reputation as the fuel for this process, since it gave off no offensive reek to spoil the flavour of the cakes. Finally they were placed in large round wicker baskets with handles at each side and stored either in the meal chest or hung from the rafters of the living room until required for use. The basket was then placed on the mantelpiece to keep the contents crisp and dry.

Thick oatcakes were also made in this region. An interesting account in the Household Book of Elizabeth Wilson of Coniston describes how wheat flour was worked into cold, stiff oatmeal porridge until the resulting dough was stiff enough to be rolled out into a 'Thick Haver Cake' about three-quarters of an inch thick. After shaping and trimming, each cake was cut into four to six portions according to its size, these then being baked on the girdle, split and buttered, and eaten hot.[34]

Bannocks

Much more common in Cumberland, however, was the use of the bannock, or jannock, a thick cake of barley, or perhaps of oat meal: 'Their bread was clap-keakk, meadd o' barley meal, Or hard havver bannock so thick'.[35]

It was this bread that Coleridge found when he entered a small cottage in the narrow valley of the River Caldew between Carrock and Bowscale Fell in the autumn of 1800. Here 'instead of the life and comfort usual in these lonely houses, I saw dirt, and every appearance of misery, a pale woman sitting by a peat fire. I asked her for bread and

milk, and she sent a child to fetch it, but she did not rise. I
ate very heartily of the black, sour bread, and drank a bowl
of milk, and asked her to permit me to pay her. "Nay" says
she, "we are not so scant as that – you are right welcome"'.[36]

The bannocks might be unleavened, the meal being
kneaded into a dough with water alone, and care being
taken not to 'Droon't miller' or 'Hang t'baker', by putting
in too much water, so that extra meal had to be borrowed
from a neighbour.[37] It was then baked on the girdle and
was turned over, perhaps using a wooden peel or 'spurtle',
in order to cook both sides evenly. Alternatively, it could
be baked amid the embers on the hearth, as a hearth or
'thar' cake before being placed on a wooden frame called
'bread-sticks' to dry out in front of the fire.

For a lighter product, a piece of fermented dough from
the previous week's baking was added to the mixture – the
sour-dough method. Bannocks made in this way using a
combination of barley and rye flour were known as Brown
George. From the later nineteenth century, artificial raising
agents began to be used to make barley bannocks, or barley
cakes, as they were now known, much more palatable. The
following recipes for this final development of the bannock
were recorded from an elderly lady by the Vicar of Alston
in 1942:[38]

Barley Cake

1 lb (450g) barley meal
1 tsp (5ml) salt
½ tsp (2.5ml) bicarbonate of soda
½ tsp (2.5ml) cream of tartar

Sufficient churn milk or buttermilk to make soft
dough; form into balls, press with the hand until the
size of a cheese plate [about 6 inches (15cm)], put
straight into the oven on a biscuit sheet [oven sheet].
Bake 20 minutes in a quick oven. They may require

turning over to brown both sides. (Break, do not cut, cakes.) [Two cakes require about ½ pt (275ml) milk and should be baked for 20 minutes at gas mark 8, 450°F (230°C)].

Barley Loaves

2 lbs (900g) Barley meal
1 lb (450g) Flour
rather less than 2 pts (1150ml) water
1 tablespoon (15ml) salt

Put meal, flour, salt into bowl, mix well, make hole in centre and add water, then add yeast which has previously risen by the fire, in half a pint (275ml) of the water stated. Mix thoroughly to a nice soft dough, cover, keep warm, set to rise in a bowl ¾ hour. Take up, form into loaves in greased tins, and set to rise ¾ of an hour, then put into brisk oven. When loaves are well risen and will turn out of tins, put on to oven shelf to brown well.

Barley Cake with Baking Powder

1 lb (450g) Barley meal
about ½ pt (275ml) old milk
1 tsp (5ml) salt
1¼ tsp (7ml) baking powder

Mix barley, salt, baking powder, and mix with the milk. Divide into 2 cakes, form into balls, pat out with hand, put on biscuit sheet [oven sheet] and bake quickly [20 minutes at gas mark 8, 450°F (230°C)].

For special occasions bannocks could be enriched in a variety of ways; made with oatmeal mixed with butter, lard, cream, or other shortening, they became moss-water cakes, and when concealing an inner layer of raisins, currants and candied peel, they became curn or double nodden cakes, eaten at kern supper [i.e. harvest supper]. Leavened bannocks also formed the basis of braftins for consumption at kern suppers. First a layer of rich cheese was spread over a yeasted bannock, these layers then being repeated four or five times. The braftin was then cut into slices and eaten with a sweet sauce flavoured with rum.[39]

Calendar Customs

As with every traditional society, the passage of each year was punctuated by a whole series of events based on Christian festivals, agricultural work, and various economic factors. Most of the calendar customs and their associated food habits practised within the Lake counties are regional variations of those found in other parts of this country. 'Easter-ledges' relate directly to the Dock-puddings of West Yorkshire, for example, just as the 'sweet-pies' are local variants on the widely-known Christmas mince pies. Comparing the available evidence with that available from elsewhere does throw up one very distinctive characteristic. Probably nowhere else in England did communal hospitality play such an important part in the lives of the people, the famous 'merry-nights' with their food and drink, stories, recitations and songs, music and dancing, card-playing and courting, providing a unique opportunity for bringing the whole community together.

The following sections each deal with a particular calendar event (excluding feasts and fairs) in which food played an important part.

New Year's Day

On the first day of the New Year, boys and girls used to go from house to house around their village singing lines such as:

> Hagmuna, Trolola,
> Give us some pie, and let us go away,

in return for which they expected to receive a pie or twopence. These gifts received, they wished the donor a happy new year, and proceeded on to the next house.[40]

93

Old Folks' Saturday

In Keswick, the first Saturday in the New Year was the day when people went to the local public houses to meet the tradesmen who had supplied them with goods throughout the previous year. Having paid their dues, they all sat down to dinner together before spending the evening in dancing, singing and good company. This appears to be a localised version of the old folks' nights at which married couples met at the main inn in the parish for a meal of roast beef, sweet pie, etc., this being followed a night or two later by a 'young folks' night' for the young and unmarried section of the community.[41]

Candlemas, February 2nd

The feast of the purification of the Virgin Mary was celebrated by eating candlemas cakes. Unfortunately no detail of their contents or method of baking appears to have survived.[42]

Collop Monday

On the Monday before Shrove Tuesday collops, slices of bacon, were fried and eaten with fried eggs, this being a survival from the medieval practice of consuming preserved fleshmeat for the last time before the onset of Lent.

Shrove Tuesday or Fasten Eve

As in other parts of the country, pancakes were eaten on this day in order to use up eggs before Lent. From now on all cooking had to be undertaken in daylight, unless the cook found her own candles; 'At Fasten Eb'n neet, Cooks find cannel leet'.[43]

Ash Wednesday

Due to the mistaken association of 'ash' with 'hash', a hash of perhaps mutton or beef might be made for the main meal on 'Hash Wednesday'.

Food in the Lake Counties

Bloody Thursday, first in Lent

In the Holme district it was customary to kill pigs on this day, their blood being used in the making of pancakes.[44]

Carling Sunday, fifth in Lent

Carlins or 'Little Godmothers' were grey peas which had been soaked in water, drained, and fried in butter or fat. In some districts the cooked peas were usually offered to visitors, while in others the raw peas were carried in the pockets to throw at friends and acquaintances. By 1878, William Dickinson commented that this custom was seldom practised in the region.[45]

Good Friday

In addition to providing an appropriate symbol of rebirth and resurrection on this great Christian springtime festival, eggs were also collected as a tithe levied at Lent and Easter in a number of Western European countries. It was remembered that Richard Birkett, priest of Martindale for sixty-seven years, used a gauge made from a piece of wood with a hole in it when collecting his Easter dues. Those eggs which passed through were rejected, and given back to the farmers.[46]

During the fortnight before Easter the price of eggs rose considerably as households decorated 'pace eggs' a name derived from 'paschal' [relating to Easter]. Various methods of decoration were employed, as described by 'Mr J.B.' of Maryport in 1825:

> A perusal of the *Every-Day Book* induces me to communicate the particulars of a custom still prevalent in some parts of Cumberland, although not as generally attended to as it was twenty or thirty years ago. I allude to the practice of sending reciprocal presents of eggs, at Easter, to the children of families respectively, betwixt whom any intimacy subsists. For some weeks preceding Good Friday the

95

price of eggs advances considerably, from the great demand occasioned by the custom referred to.

The modes adopted to prepare the eggs for presentation are the following: there may be others which have escaped my recollection.

The eggs being immersed in hot water for a few moments, the end of a common tallow-candle is made use of to inscribe the names of individuals, dates of particular events, &c. The warmth of the egg renders this a very easy process. Thus inscribed, the egg is placed in a pan of hot water, saturated with cochineal, or other dye-woods; the part over which the tallow has been passed is impervious to the operation of the dye; and consequently when the egg is removed from the pan, there appears no discolouration of the egg where the inscription has been traced, but the egg presents a white inscription on a coloured ground. The colour of course depends upon the taste of the person who prepares the egg; but usually much variety of colour is made use of.

Another method of ornamenting 'pace eggs' is, however, much neater, although more laborious, than that with the tallow-candle. The egg being dyed, it may be decorated in a very pretty manner, by means of a penknife, with which the dye may be scraped off, leaving the design white, on a coloured ground. An egg is frequently divided into compartments, which are filled up according to the taste and skill of the designer. Generally one compartment contains the name and (being young and unsophisticated) also the age of the party for whom the egg is intended. In another is, perhaps, a landscape; and sometimes a cupid is found lurking in a third: so that these 'pace eggs' become very useful auxiliaries to the missives of St Valentine. Nothing was more common in the childhood of the writer, than to see a number of these eggs preserved

96

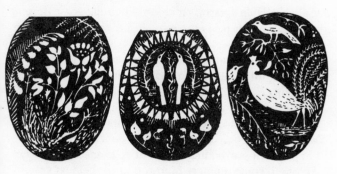

16.
These eggs, now displayed at Dove Cottage, Grasmere, were decorated between 1868 and 1878 by James Dixon, Wordsworth's gardener at Rydal Mount.

very carefully in the corner-cupboard; each egg being the occupant of a deep, long-stemmed ale-glass, through which the inscription could be read without removing it. Probably many of these eggs now remain in Cumberland, which would afford as good evidence of dates in a court of justice, as a tombstone or a family-bible.[47]

The quality of this form of decoration was quite exceptional, as may be seen in the examples decorated between 1868 and 1878 by James Dixon, Wordsworth's gardener at Rydal Mount, for the poet's grandchildren. So much time and trouble was taken in preparing these eggs that they were only given as presents to specially favoured friends or relations. Those which were to be given away to the children who called at the door were; 'simply dyed; or dotted with tallow to

present a piebald or bird's-eye appearance. These are designed for the junior boys who have not begun to participate in the pleasures of 'a bended bow and quiver full of arrows;' – a flaming torch, or a heart and a true-lover's knot. These plainer specimens are seldom promoted to the dignity of the ale-glass or the corner-cupboard.

Locally available dyestuffs included lilies and gorse flowers for yellow, onion peels for mottled browns, or ivy leaves for greens.

The children obtained their eggs by coming in groups to the door or into the kitchen, perhaps dressed in character, and singing,

> Here's two or three jolly boys all in one mind,
> We've come a pace-egging, I hope you'll prove kind,
> I hope you'll prove kind with your eggs and strong beer,
> And we'll come no more nigh you until the next year.[48]

Various characters then entered in turn, Lord Nelson, Jolly Jack Tar, Old Tosspot, and a female Old Miser with her bags, each with their appropriate lines.

In the last verse, the 'Ladies and Gentleman that sits by the fire' were requested to put their hands in their pockets and remember it was pace-egging time, after which the children received their eggs.

Other foods traditionally eaten on this day included spotted dick, especially in Eskdale, and, more generally, fig sue, a hot posset made of ale boiled with small cubes of wheaten bread and quartered figs, seasoned with sugar, treacle and nutmeg. It was considered wrong to refuse any figs offered on this day, since it was believed that Christ was crucified on a cross made of fig-wood.[49]

Easter Sunday

> On Easter Sunday we all ate Easter-ledge pudding,
> not a bad compound if the maker used only the
> white and redish stems (grown below ground) of
> that farmer's pest, the bistort or snakeweed
> (*Polygonum viviparum*). The old folks held much
> virtue in this bitter preparation, which was as good
> as a bottle of medicine, they said, and a flavouring of
> cecily (sweet bracken) was a recommendation to the
> pudding.[50]

One of the earliest detailed descriptions of this dish appeared in *The Beauties of England and Wales* of 1814, where its contents included

> the tender leaves of the alpine bistort, called here Easter-ment-gions, i.e. the sprout of the Easter month because it made its appearance about that season. Groats are the kernels of oats, divested of their inner and outer husk, and groats mixed with a small proportion of young nettles, the leaves of the great bell flower (*Campanula latifolia*) and a few blades of chives, all boiled together in a linen bag with the meat, was accounted a great delicacy to eat with veal in the spring.

The quantity and selection of fresh green herbs used in these puddings appears to have varied from household to household, depending on their individual tastes. In the following recipe, pearl barley has been substituted for groats, since they have not been readily available for most of the present century.

Easter-ledge pudding

large bunch of Easter-ledges
small bunch young nettles
1 onion, or small bunch of spring onions
4oz (100g) pearl barley
½ tsp (2.5ml) salt

Wash and clean the greens, and chop finely, mix with the barley and salt, tie up in a muslin bag and boil for 2 hours. Turn out onto a dish and season with salt, pepper and butter.

Other green ingredients could include blackcurrant, raspberry, dandelion, cabbage, lettuce, lady's mantle (*Alchemilla alpina*) leaves etc. A number of recent recipes suggest that the pudding should be beaten up in a dish with an egg and either butter or bacon-fat before serving, while others suggest the addition of a little vinegar.

Easter Monday

This was the great day for families to gather together at some traditional local meeting-place in order to hold individual competitions with their eggs. Up to 1,500 children used to come to Kendal's Castle Hill for this purpose late last century. Here pairs of children sat opposite each other across a stretch of level turf, then trundled their eggs one against another until one was broken and forfeited to the winner, who would probably eat it then and there.[51] On the steep sloping Easter Field at Clifton, or the Castle Moat at Penrith, meanwhile, the children rolled their eggs down together, running after them to find the winner, whose egg was last to break. Around the Solway, the competition took a different form, each youth:

> Holding his egg in his hand challenges a companion to give blow for blow. One of the eggs is sure to be broken, and its shattered remains are the spoil of the conqueror: who is instantly invested with the title of 'a cock of one, two, three,' &c. in proportion as it may have fractured his antagonist's eggs in the conflict. A successful egg, in a contest with one which had previously gained honours, adds to its number the reckoning of its vanquished foe. An egg which is a 'cock' of ten or a dozen, is frequently challenged.[52]

Court Leet Dinners

The court leet was the customary court of a manor, at which the bailiff and the steward, assisted by a jury of local men, determined matters relating to the occupation of copyhold lands, the enclosure of commons, etc. At the

opening of the present century these courts still followed
their medieval routines, but their days were numbered;
most of their functions were terminated in 1912 when, by
Act of Parliament, copyhold tenure was abolished.
Fortunately A. W. Rumney has recorded how one Lakeland
court functioned during its latter days, although the style
of its catering suggests that little had changed over the
previous 150 years.[53] On this occasion the court met in the
upper room of an inn at eleven o'clock on a late June
morning, and managed to conclude its business within the
hour, so that everyone could be seated at table downstairs
by noon. The steward then carved a huge joint of roast
beef, which was accompanied by pease pudding and new
potatoes. Everyone was then given a glass of raw brandy
with which to toast 'The King, God bless him!', and the
final course of plum pudding was served. After the meal
had ended, those attending the court were asked to pay a
shilling (5p) 'colt money' for further drinks, the steward
adding five shillings (25p) on the lord's behalf, and the
bailiff twenty-four shillings (£1.20) for the jurymen. The
toast to 'The Lord of the Manor' was then proposed, as
donor of the feast, to which the steward responded before
finally proposing 'The Jury'. Now that all formal business
had been concluded, the party entered into song before
breaking up and returning to their respective homes.

Clipping

Around midsummer the sheep were brought down from
the fells for washing in a dammed-up stream, the washers
frequently resorting to whisky to keep out the effects of
the cold water. About two weeks later the flocks were
gathered again for clipping. This was a communal affair,
all those who kept sheep in the area meeting at each farm
in turn in order that each flock could be clipped in a single
day. Up to around the middle of the nineteenth century the
clipping ended with a bare-foot race for a fleece mounted
on a pole, followed by a dinner and an evening of

celebration, during which the shepherd was chaired by the party. A good impression of a traditional clipping is given in W. Dickinson's poem 'Cumbriana';

Now clippin' o' done, comes weshin' o' hands
    And kestin' off scoggers and brats;
A fleece is hung up on a powl in t' lang-lands,
    To be run for without shun or hats.

The prize is awarded, to feastin' they wend,
    At a plain but a plentiful spreed;
On broad pewder dishes, weel leadden at t' end,
    Wood trunchers off whilk they can feed.

Next out wid a punch bowl, and yal i' girt plenty,
    Wi' horns and glasses to drink frae;
And piggins, and mugs, but nought varra dainty,
    And nought 'at a clipper need shrink frae.

Than a whyat laal crack for about hoaf an hour,
    And a buzz – seun to rise till a chang;
Than somebody knattles on t' teable befooor
    He says, 'Lads, you mun join in my sang'.

*'Here's a good health to the man o' this house,
    'The man o' this house, the man o' this house;
'Here's a good health to the man o' this house,
    'For he is a right honest man.

'And he that doth this health deny,
    'Before his face I justify [or just defy];
'Right in his face this glass shall fly,
    'So let this health go round.

'Place the canny cup to your chin,
    'Open your mouth and let liquor run in;
'The more you drink the fuller your skin,
    'So let this health go round.'

Than 'O good ale thou are my darlin',’
   And t' shepherds' 'Tarry woo;’
'The Raven and the Rock Starlin',’
   And many a ringer too.

To help a good neighbour at his merry meetin',
   A heall country side to employ;
In housin' and clippin' wi' much friendly greetin',
   For clippin's are meetin's o' joy.

(*A very old clipping song. The guests in turn obey the commands of the seventh verse, and if the glass is not emptied by the end of the refrain, the penalty is enforced a second time. And if a man was desirous to get quickly drunk, he would incur the penalty till his end was accomplished.)

Early this century, the clippers might gather around eleven o'clock in the morning and work through to around two in the afternoon. They then washed and went in to the house where a glass of ale and a little heap of oatcake was set at each place on the long covered table. The host began to slice the smoking-hot round of beef, which his womenfolk then dished up with pease-pudding, potatoes boiled in their skins, and Yorkshire pudding for each guest. This was followed by boiled puddings, perhaps plain, or gooseberry, etc., served with strongly-flavoured rum sauce, all eaten with carefully-wiped knives and forks retained from the first course. By three o'clock the clippers were back at work once more, pint mugs of tea with big hunches of gooseberry pasty and tea-cake being served to each man later, at intervals between the clipping of pairs of sheep. Around seven in the evening, with the day's work completed, everyone washed and returned to the house once more, where the table was laid with the cold beef and mashed potatoes retained from dinner, now served with saucers of pickled onions and cabbage. Cheese then took the place of a pudding, after which pipes and glasses of spirits were circulated, and the singing began.[54]

Rushbearing Gingerbreads

When most churches in this region were still unpaved, they were made cool and fragrant in summer and warm and dry in winter by having a layer of field rushes spread across their floors. Once they were properly floored, the practical need for furnishing the churches in this way disappeared entirely; but in a number of Westmorland villages the customs of bringing rushes into the church and of making decorative 'burdens' of rushes and flowers were retained as major festivals. On a Saturday, usually the one nearest the feast days of the church's patron saint, August 5th for St Oswald at Grasmere, for example, and June 29th for St Peter at Warcop (despite its dedication to St Columba!) colourful processions bearing both large formal burdens made by the adults and smaller less formal burdens made by the children walked around the village before returning to the rush-strewn church for a service.[55]

The traditional gift from the church to the rush-bearers took the form of a piece of gingerbread, the Grasmere churchwardens' accounts of 1819 recording the payment of 3s 9d (19p) for 'Rushbearers' Gingerbread'. Similar payments continued to be made up to 1858, and then for some years the gingerbread was no longer provided; but since 1871, when the custom was revived, a gingerbread bearing the stamp of St Oswald has been given to each bearer every year. Late last century it was baked by the Walker family who ran the village shop. They were followed in succession from around 1913 to 1938 by Mrs Mary Dixon of Townend, Miss Sarah Hodgson and Miss Gibson, after which it was supplied by Mr J. J. Foster.[56] A similar custom survives at Ambleside, but the ginger beer and ginger biscuits remembered at Warcop in the 1880s now appear to be a thing of the past.

Pea Scaldings

Peas were one of the few vegetables regularly grown in this region, as described in the following account;

Pease. – In a climate where so much rain falls, and where the harvest is so precarious, the culture of pease would be attended with so many chances of loss, and so few of gain, that we were not surprized to find them so generally neglected. The difficulty of harvesting them, has probably first suggested the idea of building their stacks in the cloughs of trees, and afterwards in slender high pyramids round the boles of tall trees, to prevent them from blowing over: by this method they can also lead and stack them in a damper or moister state; and as they do not come near the ground by five or six feet, they are seldom troubled with mice. The greatest diameter of the stacks is not more than six or seven feet; the height of many twelve or fifteen; if the tree has not a sufficiency of convenient branches to bear the bottom, they nail a stick or two across, to form a base. When finished, they have a very singular appearance.[57]

A sheaf of peas brought down from one of these stacks could form the basis of brazzled peas in northern and eastern Cumberland.[58] It was first carried to the village green, when the halms were readily set alight. As the flames subsided, the local boys went down on their hands and knees amongst the hot ashes, seeking the hidden treasure. The peas, some still green, some only scorched, and others charred to a cinder, were all excellent in their opinion, and they only gave up the search when every pea had been consumed, their hands and faces being as black as sweeps' at the end of the scramble.

Pea scaldings were popular entertainments, either on their own, or as part of a kern supper. Jamie Muckelt of Crosthwaite erecting the following notice in his pea-field early last century, in order to discourage people from helping themselves;

> 'Pray ye, nebbers, dunnot pull;
> I'll gi' ye a pey-scode when they're full
> If ye eat 'em when they're swash
> They'll fill your belly full o' trash.[59]

For the scalding, the young grey peas were boiled in the pod, thrown into a riddle or an oval swill basket to drain, and served with a cup of melted butter in the middle. Each person then took a pod, dipped it in the butter, stripped it in his mouth, and pelted the others with the swad.

> A scowdin o' pez they set up in a swill,
> An bade t' em all eat till they brust, man,
> Now coloured wi' pepper, an' han'fuls o' sawt,
> In basons of butter they thrust, man.
> Sweethearts are serious, an wheyles they like fun,
> They pelted each other wi' swads, man,
> Such feightin' girt Bonnyprat niver yance seed
> Stone-blind in a crack wer' the lads, man![60]

The Mell

On cutting the last sheaf of corn, it was usually plaited to enclose a large apple, and hung up in the farm kitchen until Christmas Day, when the corn was given to the best cow, and the apple to the oldest farm servant.[61]

Kern Supper

The Kern Supper or, in northern Cumberland, the Kernwinnin, was the harvest-home supper, held in the corn-lands of the north and west when all the grain crops had been harvested. This feast gained its name from the kirn, or churn, which held the thick cream which, with oat or wheaten cake, formed the final dish of the evening.

In the early evening, the harvesters gathered around the white-clothed table in the barn where the priests said grace, and the meal was served;

Harvest gets endit like meast other things,
    And kern-supper follows as sure;
A thanksgiving feast contentment still brings,
    If a morsel be spared to the poor.

Than hey! for thick bannocks and rich butter sops,
    Wid iv'ry thing dainty and nice;
T' maister says, 'Fettle tee, lads, we've good crops,'
    And neabody needs preezin' twice.

To piggins o' frummety [barley and milk],
    And bannocks and butter to follow;
And sops so smeath 'at they slip down like silk,
    They bang watter poddish clean hollow.

Than t' breet pewder dishes begin to leuk howe,
    And mickle mair cannot weel spend;
And youngsters 'll stritch their arms – some scrat
                       their powe,
    Ilk yan o' them full to t' thropple end.[62]

To close the meal, apricots, cherries, nuts and the cream might be served, then the 'great ones' had wine and the poor their rum, and dancing commenced to the music of the fiddle.

A little later, an eight-pint punch bowl was brought in, the priest giving a toast such as 'Of peace, health and plenty, while England exists' or 'May canny aul' Cummerlan' boast' before the contents were consumed.

At midnight, the feast continued with a scalding of peas. Numerous songs and other entertainments such as recitations and stories then followed, the punch-bowl being refilled as necessary, with the usual consequence that fighting broke out. In the early hours, with the floor awash with blood and punch, the candles went out, leaving the survivors in the dark until dawn, when they made their way home with broken bones and bloody faces.[63]

Most of the dishes served at the Kern Supper also

appeared at other communal festivities, during the course of the year. Buttered sops, chiefly served in central and northern Cumberland, were made by soaking wheat or oat bread in ale, melted butter and sugar, the whole being worked into a solid mass and eaten with a spoon. Around Allonby they were called buttered crumbs, if no ale was included in the mixture.[64]

Frumety was made by soaking whole wheat in water until the husks were swollen, after which they were gently beaten with a wooden pestle in a stone mortar, known in north-west Cumberland as a knocking-trough and elsewhere as a creeing trough, until the husks came free, and could be rinsed off. The soaked wheat was then slowly cooked with milk, sugar, and perhaps spices, rum or flour to flavour or thicken it, depending on each household's taste and means. Cumberland was one of the few counties which retained frumety as an everyday winter-time dish to accompany savoury food, just as it had been in the medieval period. Evidence for this is given in the lines describing February, in William Dickinson's *Cumbriana* of 1876:

> Sum wheat mun be cree't for a frummety dish,
> In t' creein trough, 'back o' t' lathe door;
> A piggin o' that with a bit o' salt fish,
> Maks a dinner for rich or for poor'.

Barring-Out (September or October)

At this time of year the master was locked out of his school by the scholars, who refused to let him enter until he had signed an agreement setting out the holidays for the coming year. Once this had been done, the doors were opened so that everyone could enjoy a meal of beef, beer and wine. Alternatively a subscription would be raised for supplies of ale, fruit, and wheat bread as a special luxury. In some parts of the region barring-out took place at other times of the year, Shrove Tuesday being the traditional day at Bromfield, for example.[65]

Sergeant Monday

Before the Reform Act of 1835, the borough of Kendal enjoyed two mayoral banquets each year, the old mayor holding his on the last Monday in September, while the new mayor gave his after being sworn in on the first Monday in October. As the *Westmorland Advertiser and Kendal Chronicle* reported, when Joseph Swainson took office in 1827, the long-established custom of scrambling for apples took place as usual;

> In the morning the children of all the schools assembled in the streets and accompanied by the Mayor's Sergeants proceeded to the residence of the worthy gentleman where a very large quantity of apples etc., were distributed amongst them. In the scraffle for the fruit several of the boys displayed great adroitness and dexterity.

In 1829 the *Westmorland Advertiser* noted the 'pecks of apples showered upon the heads (of the children) from the windows of the Town Hall while hundreds of urchins below scrambled, shouted, and seemed happy'. After the Reform Act there were attempts to continue the custom, but the whole affair got completely out of control, Thomas Hall, teacher of the British School in Castle Street, having to fight a running battle with two or three hundred of the roughest lads in the town until he finally agreed to let his boys join in the proceedings, scraffling for nuts thrown from the Town Hall. From this time, the robust celebration of Sergeant Monday became a thing of the past.[66]

Christmas

> At Christmas, when the greatest hospitality prevails among the villagers, every family is provided with goose pies, minced pies and ale. Where flocks of sheep are kept, there is also an ancient custom of killing the fattest among them before Christmas. Of

this they make the first meal for breakfast on
Christmas-day, which consists of minced meat, made
rich with fruit, and boiled in the ventricle of the
animal.[67]

'A Gentleman in Cumberland' contributed details of this
dish to Richard Bradley's *Country Housewife and Lady's
Director* of 1736 (p. 122);

It is a custom with us every Christmas-Day in the
Morning to have, what we call an Hackin, for the
Breakfast of the young Men who work about our
House; and if this Dish is not dressed by that time it
is Day-light, the Maid is led through the Town,
between two Men, as fast as they can run with her,
up Hill and down Hill, which she accounts a great
shame. But as for the Receipt to make this Hackin,
which is admired so much by us, it is as follows.
Take the Bag or Paunch of a Calf, and wash it,
and clean it well with Water and Salt; then take
some Beef-Suet, and shred it small, and shred some
Apples, after they are pared and cored, very small.
Then put in some Sugar, and some Spice beaten
small, a little Lemon-Peel cut very fine, and a little
Salt, and a good quantity of Grots, or whole Oatmeal, steep'd a Night in Milk; then mix these all
together, and add as many Currans pick'd clean from
the Stalks, and rubb'd in a coarse Cloth; but let
them not be washed. And when you have all ready,
mix them together, and put them into the Calf's
Bag, and tye them up, and boil them till they are
enough. You may, if you will, mix up with the
whole, some Eggs beaten, which will help to bind it.
This is our Custom to have ready, at the opening of
the Doors, on Christmas Day in the Morning. It is
esteem'd here; but all that I can say to you of it, is,
that it eats somewhat like a Christmas-Pye, or is

110

somewhat like that boil'd. I had forgot to say, that
with the rest of the Ingredients, there should be
some Lean of tender Beef minced small.

This sweet variety of the haggis, known locally as a
hackin, appears to have largely disappeared by the 1870s, its
place being taken by the 'sweet pie', which consisted of the
same basic ingredients baked beneath a thick pastry crust
instead of being boiled in a sheep's stomach.[68] Perhaps this
change reflects the widespread introduction of cast-iron
kitchen ranges with ovens which had just taken place. A
typical recipe for the sweet pie is given in the *Cumberland
Women's Institute Cookery Book*;

Pastry:

2lb (900g) flour
1lb (450g) lard
4oz (125g) butter
pinch of salt

Filling:

8oz (225g) currants
8oz (225g) raisins
8oz (225g) best mutton
8oz (225g) sugar
½oz (15g) lemon peel
2 large apples
½ nutmeg, grated
½ tsp (2.5ml) ground cinnamon
½ glass (30ml) rum
½ gill (100ml) ale

Chop all the filling finely and mix together before
putting into a large pie dish. Roll out the pastry
thickly to cover the dish, decorate, and bake for some
2 hours at gas mark 4, 350°F (180°C). The filling
must boil during cooking.

Other pies might be made of mutton or of goose, the offal of the latter being used to make giblet pies, for which the giblets were enriched with black puddings of goose or pig blood mixed with finely-shredded unrendered lard, shelled oats, and a seasoning of corn-mint.

The period between Christmas Day and Twelfth Night was the traditional time for lively parties or 'merry-nights' held either in ale-houses or in private homes. The host laid in stocks of ale, bread, cheese, spirits, pipes, tobacco and musicians. Once everyone had come together, probably around 7 pm after milking and other domestic duties had been finished, the young women had pies set before them to eat, after which the party divided into groups, depending on their particular interests – card players retiring to a room equipped with a fire and large tables, sweethearts into some snug secluded corner and the dancers up the ladder into the loft. Here they tended to exhibit vitality and agility, rather than polished Terpsichorean skill, heads frequently bumping the rafters as the dashing fiddle music gave activity, if not grace, to the big unwieldy limbs of the Cumbrian dancers. At the end of each jig the fiddler made his instrument squeak out two notes which said 'Kiss her!', which everyone did with a resounding smack on the lips, similar to the crack of a waggoner's whip. Downstairs, meanwhile, the drinkers sat in the kitchen or bower until dawn.[69]

Wordsworth describes one of these events in his 'Waggoner'

> 'Blithe and lightsome hearts have we
> Feasting at the *Cherry Tree*!
> What bustling, jostling, high and low!
> A universal overflow!
> What tankards foaming from the tap,
> What store of cakes in every lap,
> What thumping, stamping overhead,
>   The thunder had not been more busy:

> With such a stir you could have said
>   The little place may well be dizzy
> 'Tis who can dance with greatest vigour
> 'Tis what can be most prompt and eager
> As if it heard the fiddle's call
> The pewter clatters on the wall;
> The very bacon shows its feeling,
> Swinging from the smoky ceiling'.

A further description of these events in the 1820s describes how the dancing finished around midnight 'when they sit down to lobscouse and pousoudie; the former made of beef, potatoes and onions fried together; and pousoudie . . . [made] of ale boiled with sugar and nutmeg into which are put roasted apples'.[70] The pousoudie, which could also be made with ale, spirits and spices was usually served up in large communal bowls called doublers, into which everyone dipped their spoons, although in the more prosperous houses a posset-cup with two, three or more tubular spouts enabled the drinkers to suck pousoudie directly up into their mouths.[71]

In some instances, the substantial quantities of food and drink consumed at these merry nights was paid for by subscription:

> two women are chosen, who with wooden bowls
> placed one within the other so as to leave an opening
> and a space between them go round to the female
> part of the society in succession, and what one puts
> into the uppermost bowl the collectress slips into the
> bowl beneath it. All are expected to contribute
> something, but not more than a shilling, and they
> are best esteemed who give most. The men choose
> two from themselves, and follow the same custom,
> except as the gentlemen are not supposed to be
> altogether so fair in their dealings as the ladies, one

113

of the collectors is furnished with pen, ink and paper
to set down the subscriptions as soon as received.[72]

Thus, with the end of the merry nights on Twelfth Night,
the annual cycle of festivities was ready to begin once more.

***Notes and
References***

1. J. Housman, *A Topographical Description of Cumberland,
Westmoreland* . . . (Carlisle, 1800), pp. 68–70.
2. W. Hutchinson, *The History of the County of Cumberland*
(Carlisle, 1794), pp. 546; 574; 570; 525; 521.
3. W. Rollinson, *Life & Tradition in the Lake District* (London,
1974), pp. 102–3.
4. W. Wilberforce, *Journey to the Lake District 1779* (Stocksfield,
1983), p. 55.
5. D. Scott, *Bygone Cumberland & Westmorland* (London, 1899),
p. 218.
6. D. Wordsworth, *Journal*, 16th June 1800.
7. J. Nicolson & R. Burn, *The History and Antiquities of the
Counties of Westmorland and Cumberland* (London, 1777), p. 7;
T. W. Palmer, *English Lakeland* (London, 1905), p. 117.
8. Scott (1899), p. 217.
9. T. W. Thompson, *Wordsworths, Hawkshead* (Oxford, 1970),
p. 86.
10. Rollinson (1974), p. 93; Hutchinson (1794), p. 521.
11. W. Dickinson, *A Glossary of Words and Phrases pertaining to the
Dialect of Cumberland* (London, 1878), 'batten sticks'.
12. A. W. Rumney, *The Dalesman* (Kendal, 1936), p. 165.
13. Dickinson (1878), 'bullens'.
14. J. Greenop, 'A Contrivance for making fire . . .' *Trans.
Cumberland & Westmorland Antiquarian & Archaeological
Society*, N.S.7 (1907), p. 207.
15. J. Gough, *The Manners & Customs of Westmorland* (Kendal,
1847), pp. 12–13.
16. E. E. Evans, *Irish Folk Ways* (London, 1957), pp. 62; 93.
17. R. Brunskill, *Vernacular Architecture of the Lake Counties*
(London, 1974), pp. 51; 130.
18. M. Denwood & T. W. Thompson, *eds., A Lafter o 'Farleys*
(Kendal, 1950), p. 40.
19. These are now in the Museum of Lakeland Life & Industry,
Kendal.
20. B. L. Thompson *ed. Westmorland Villages* (Kendal, 1957), pp.
75; 105.
21. Brotherton Library, University of Leeds, MS 432/4, pp. 102–6.
22. Housman (1800), p. 79.
23. A. Pringle, *General View of the Agriculture of the County of
Westmorland* (Edinburgh, 1794), p. 337.
24. Denwood & Thompson (1950), pp. 74; 117.

25. D. Wordsworth, *Journal*, 22nd December 1801 & 17th May 1800.
26. W. Dickinson, *Cumbriana* (London, 1876), p. 99.
27. Dickinson (1878), 'oot'.
28. Dickinson (1878), 'bicker'.
29. Brotherton Library, MS 432/4, p. 68.
30. C. Fiennes, *Journeys*, ed. C. Morris (London, 1949), pp. 193-4.
31. *Lonsdale Magazine* 3 (1822), p. 325.
32. Pringle (1794), p. 337.
33. Brotherton Library, MSS 432/3, pp. 26; 99-103; 432/4, pp. 4; 13; 72.
34. Thompson (1957), p. 103.
35. *Dialect Poems, Songs & Ballads* (London, 1839), 'clapbread'.
36. G. S. Sandilands, *The Lakes* (London, 1947), p. 19. Letter from S. T. Coleridge to Sir Humphry Davy, 18th October, 1800.
37. Dickinson (1878), 'Droon t'Miller'.
38. Brotherton Library, MS 432/3, p. 17.
39. Dickinson (1878), 'Moss-watter ceakk'; R. Anderson, *Cumbrian Ballads* (Carlisle, 1864), p. 196.
40. Anderson (1864); J. Sullivan, *Cumberland and Westmorland Ancient and Modern* (London, Kendal, 1857), p. 170.
41. *Journal, Lakeland Dialect Society*, 33 (1971), p. 22, reprinted from a *West Cumberland Times* article of 1897. See also Dickinson (1878), 'Oald Fwock's Neet'.
42. Sullivan (1857), p. 163.
43. Palmer (1905), p. 56; Dickinson (1878), 'Fasten Eve'.
44. Dickinson (1878), 'Bloody Thursday'.
45. Sullivan (1857), p. 164; J. Murray, *Handbook to Westmorland, Cumberland and the Lakes* (London, 1869); R. Ferguson, *Northmen* (London, 1856), p. 208.
46. W. R. Mitchell, *Men of Lakeland* (London, 1966), p. 83; Sullivan (1857), p. 164.
47. W. Hone, *The Everyday Book*, 2 vols. (London, 1826-27), I, pp. 426-8; II, p. 450.
48. Sullivan (1857), p. 164.
49. Rollinson (1974), p. 52; *Dialect Poems, Songs and Ballads* (1839); Dickinson (1878), 'Figsue'.
50. W. T. Palmer, *Odd Yarns of English Lakeland* (London, 1914), p. 33.
51. Thompson (1957), p. 34; V. Newall, *An Egg at Easter* (London, 1971), p. 339.
52. Hone (1826), I, pp. 426-8.
53. Rumney (1936), pp. 82-95.
54. *ibid.*, pp. 105-115.
55. P. Brears, *Northcountry Folk Art* (Edinburgh, 1989), pp. 182-9.
56. E. F. Rawnsley, *The Rushbearing in Grasmere & Ambleside* (London, 1953), p. 25.
57. J. Bailey & G. Culley, *General View of the Agriculture of the County of Cumberland* (London, c. 1850), p. 221.

58. Dickinson (1878), 'Brazzled Pez'.
59. L. Turvar, *Tales & Legends of the English Lakes* (London, c. 1850), p. 237.
60. Anderson (1864), p. 280.
61. Dickinson (1878), 'Mell'.
62. Dickinson (1876), p. 250.
63. Anderson (1864), p. 280.
64. *Dialect Poems* (1839), p. 280; Dickinson (1878), 'butter sops'.
65. Hone (1826), I, pp. 402–8; *Dialect Poems* (1839), 'Barring-Out'.
66. E. M. Wilson, 'Some Extinct Kendal Customs', *Trans. Cumberland & Westmorland Antiquarian & Archaeological Society*, N.S. 38 (1938), pp. 164–72.
67. F. Jollie, *Sketch of Cumberland Manners and Customs* (Carlisle, 1811), p. 43.
68. Dickinson (1878), 'Hackin'.
69. R. Anderson, *Anderson's Cumberland Ballads* (Carlisle, 1864), p. 188.
70. Hone (1826), I, p. 53.
71. J. Gough, *The Manners & Customs of Westmorland* (Kendal, 1847), p. 24.
72. Hone (1826), I, p. 53.

5.

Lancashire's Heritage

HELEN POLLARD

Despite the popular image, Lancashire is not all dark satanic mills. It is true man has disfigured the countryside with mills, mines, slagheaps and slums, but nearly three quarters of the country is still a green and pleasant land. The west of the county is bounded by the sea, the south by the flat fields of Cheshire. The northern and eastern boundaries are formed by mountains, to the north the lakeland fells, to the east the Pennine hills. Before the 1974 reorganisation, the little known area of Furness, with its own special character, was part of the county as well.

The Fylde and the area around Ormskirk were once marshland and moss. Today, as a result of drainage and modern agricultural methods, a wide variety of vegetables are grown commercially, notably tomatoes. Further inland, owing to the hilly countryside and high rainfall, sheep- and cattle-rearing were more important in the past than crops, and by Tudor times, unlike most of England, farms were generally enclosed. The terrain and climate also determined the crops which were grown, oats and rye being more suitable than wheat. The poor soils of the area made it necessary for the owners of small farms to have an extra source of income, and so many men combined the hand-weaving of woollen fabrics with agricultural work, the women undertaking the less physically demanding spinning of the yarn. The working day was long, maximum use having to be made of daylight; therefore easily prepared dishes, which could be left to cook unattended were popular. There are records of farmworkers taking a

17.
Map of Lancashire.

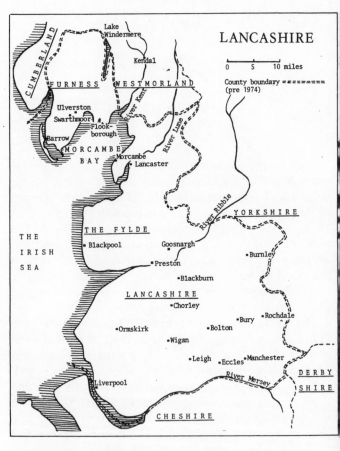

steaming pot with them to the fields and burying it in a haystack until needed, thus anticipating the haybox cooker!

The industrial areas are limited to the south east of the county around Liverpool and Manchester. Coal has been mined for centuries. The Pennines provided stone for building and other trades established in the county included glass, paper, soap, hardware and ordnance. Cotton, however, was king in Lancashire. During the nineteenth century woollen manufacture was superseded by cotton

118

and the chief cotton industry in the world became established in Lancashire. In 1901 out of 483,000 operatives employed in England in the cotton manufacturing industry 399,000 were working in Lancashire. The high relative humidity is often quoted as the reason for cotton's dominance, but there were others just as important.

Lancashire's woollen products from the rough Pennine sheep were not up to the quality of that of other centres, and so the Lancashire textile workers were not subject to the strict guild controls of the woollen industry. In 1700 and 1701, Acts were passed banning the import of cotton cloth which was becoming popular owing to the fashion of lighter clothing. These Acts benefitted the fledgling Lancashire cotton industry, as no mention was made of the cloth which was being produced in Lancashire. The seaboard faced the New World, and ports at Preston, Liverpool and Lancaster were convenient for imports of raw cotton from the West Indies and the cotton states of America. Fast-flowing Pennine streams and, later, coal were readily available for power. The development of railways ensured good internal communications. For most of the eighteenth century the textile labourer prospered owing to the increasing demand for cotton fabrics, and the first machines invented favoured the hand textile workers, but later inventions started the gradual change to factory production. Industrialisation and other factors such as land enclosure, the Napoleonic wars, the Corn Laws and the American Civil War resulted in a steady decline of the textile workers' living standards during the first half of the nineteenth century. In 1800 a hand loom weaver's average wage was thirty shillings (£1.50) a week, by 1820 it was fourteen shillings (70p) eventually dropping as low as one penny (½p) per hour.

In 1832 Dr James Kay described the life of a Manchester textile operative.[1] He rose at 5 am, worked from 6 am to 8 am and then returned home for half an hour for breakfast of tea or coffee and a little bread. Work resumed until noon when he had an hour for dinner, the poorer worker dining on boiled potatoes and a little melted lard or a few pieces of fried fat bacon, the better off on potatoes and a small amount of meat. Work then continued until 7 pm followed by supper of tea and bread. Other reports present a similar picture.[2]

Tea, bread, porridge, potatoes, cheese and perhaps a little bacon constituted the usual diet which in times of hardship was reduced to tea, bread and porridge. Even when the workers could afford a more varied diet, many wives had little time or energy for cooking as they worked in the factories as well, and so simple dishes that would not spoil if left on the hob all day were as popular with the mill workers as they had been with the farmers. Low wages and rising costs meant cheaper cuts of meat and offal had to be used. Fortunately these respond well to long, slow, moist cooking which has a tenderising effect on tough connective tissue. Offal such as heads, trotters, tripe and cow heel was not in demand and so could be purchased cheaply and add variety to the diet. Overcrowded living conditions in back-to-back houses built round a yard with a stand pipe and communal privy, houses often lacking cooking facilities other than an open fire, led to the rise of cooked meat shops, pie shops and, later, fish and chip shops where the housewife could buy a tasty meal for her family at the end of the working day. I can still remember cooked-meat shops in Bury in the 1940s. One in particular I can recall with scrubbed wooden tables and high backed benches. The food was cooked in the basement, mainly large roasted joints and pies in huge metal dishes the size of washing up bowls. The tradition of these shops lives on in markets, which are the best places to find regional foods and encounter the quality and humour of the Lancashire workers.

Sweet and usually richer dishes, using the more expensive ingredients such as butter, spices and dried fruits are still baked in farmhouse kitchens and can be bought in many towns and villages. Many of these dishes are associated with special occasions when there would have been a rare holiday to break the monotony of daily work. At times such as these a little extravagance could be allowed to purchase fairings.

The pattern of the working day inevitably influenced meals as well. Because of the long working hours early rising was essential. Breakfast dishes needed to be quick and easy to prepare – bread, oatmeal porridge, tea with a cooked dish such as fried bacon, black pudding or sausages if these could be afforded. Usually there was not sufficient time to return home at midday so workers patronised the cooked meat shops or took food to the mill. Hot dishes were kept warm on the boiler and pipes of the steam engines, a practice still continuing within living memory. Tea became an important meal. The working housewife would rely on cooked meats or food from the cook shop unless she had left a pot simmering all day. In the better-off homes there would be a generous spread; a hot dish or a variety of cold meats and pickles, bread and butter, cakes and pastries. Many of Lancashire's traditional dishes can only be found today as recipes or descriptions in books and, interesting though they are to read, it is not always possible to recreate them exactly, as quality of ingredients, methods of production and cooking facilities have changed. However, during the years I lived in Lancashire and during more recent visits, I have found a number of them either on sale or being cooked in the home and I shall now consider in greater detail some foods which are available today and others which have disappeared.

In Lancashire the growing of wheat took second place to oats as the cool climate is not ideally suited to the growing of wheat and, in addition, much of the ground is too stony.

Bread and oatcakes

Avena Vesca, common Otes, is called Vesca, a Vescendo, because it is used in many countries to make sundry sorts of bread, as in Lancashire, where it is the chiefest bread corne for Jannocks, Haver cakes, Tharffe cakes, and for those which are called generally Oten cakes; and for the most part they call the graine Haver, whereof they do likewise make drinke for want of Barley.[3]

Oats, unlike wheat, are deficient in gluten and so are not suitable for making bread. In addition many cottages and houses lacked ovens, so the oats were used to make oatcakes.

Unlike Scottish oatcakes, the oatcakes are soft and floppy when first made. A slightly leavened batter is used, leavening being achieved by (1) yeast (2) buttermilk (3) leaving the batter overnight to ferment naturally (c.f. haver-cake in Yorkshire, haver being derived from Old Norse *hafrar*, meaning 'oats'). If not eaten at once the cakes would be dried and stored draped over wooden beams or lines. Dried oatcake forms part of the dish *Stew and 'ard* a popular dish in pubs around Burnley. Stew was a kind of pressed meat or *brawn* made from cheap cuts of meat such as shin beef, cooked slowly to gelatinise the tough connective tissue, then set in a mould to form a jelly. 'Ard was dried oatcakes or fresh oatcakes toasted until slightly crisp. Oatmeal is also used for *Throdkin*, a filling savoury dish of oatmeal, lard and water topped by bacon rashers and baked in the oven.

Barm cakes   Barm is the name given to the froth that forms on the top of malt liquor, and it was used before compressed or German yeast was available to leaven bread (from OE *Beorma*). Barm cakes are round soft bread rolls also known as oven bottoms, as they are baked on the flat base of the bread oven. In Lancashire they are the preferred bread for sandwiches and many shops and market stalls sell them with a wide variety of fillings.

Blackley muffins are a recent development, being the

brain child of Bill and Sam Ward. They had the novel idea of colouring their muffins during a local municipal election, red for Labour, yellow for Liberal, blue for Conservative. Now muffins are made for all local and general elections and in addition were made for the 1975 Common Market referendum, sales of them giving, so it is claimed, a very good indication of the outcome of an election.

Many traditional dishes of Lancashire feature potatoes in their ingredients, for example, hotpot, lobscouse, meat and potato pie, potato cakes, fish and chips and chip butties. Potatoes had become established in Ireland between 1580 and 1600. How they were first introduced into Lancashire is not clear but tradition says an Irish ship was wrecked off the coast, and amongst the stores washed ashore were potatoes. Whatever the truth of this story, by 1680 potatoes were established in Lancashire (the first recorded instance of potatoes as a garden crop in the north being in 1673 at Swarthmoor Hall, Ulverston, the home of the Quaker Fell family, who were friends and protectors of George Fox). It is claimed potatoes were as popular in Lancashire as in Ireland, putting the county ahead of the rest of England by at least a century.

Potatoes

As to why this happened in Lancashire rather than other parts of England, Redcliffe Salaman gives several reasons:
Potato cultivation was favoured by:
1. the system of land tenure – in Lancashire small holdings each with their own enclosed fields had replaced the open field system where the common right of post-harvest grazing did not favour late root crops;
2. the deep moss soils and moist climate;
3. the position of the textile worker – at that time, due to the increasing demand for cotton, he was relatively the best paid and fed in England, and
     had the opportunity and leisure to cultivate his own

123

land in such a manner as to lend itself best to the support of himself and his family. The potato used in this manner allowed the worker greater freedom to purchase more expensive foods.[4]

Edward Hyams advances another reason:

the Lancashire worker was an industrial worker: it has been shown time and time again that an industrial proletariat is far more intelligent, far more ready and anxious to get an education, read books; far quicker to throw off old superstitions and prejudices than a peasantry.[5]

Whatever the reasons, potatoes are widely used in Lancashire dishes. Perhaps the best known is *hotpot*. A special deep, straight-sided earthenware pot is used as originally the dish was made with mutton chops which were stood up on end round the base of the pot. A deep pot was needed to accommodate the long rib bones of large Pennine sheep. The pot would then be filled with layers of potatoes and onions and a little water added, and it was left, covered, in the oven or on the side of the hob to cook slowly all day, providing a hot nourishing meal for the farmer's or worker's return. The dish would be served with pickled red cabbage or beetroot. *Lobscouse* or lobby is a dish with a long history. It was originally a shipboard stew of salt meat, ships biscuits and any available vegetables. The derivation of the word is unknown, according to the Oxford English Dictionary, but similar words exist in Northern European languages such as 'labskaus' (Germany) and 'lapskojs' (Sweden). In Lancashire it is made with pieces of beef or mutton, onions and perhaps other root vegetables cooked in a pot or pan, barley sometimes being added to echo the ships biscuits. Lobscouse is especially associated with Liverpool, and probably gave rise to the Liverpudlian nickname 'scouse'. *Meat and potato pie* or *potato pie* is still a popular dish at socials and Sunday

School events as it is tasty, filling and cheap, large potato pie dishes of a similar shape to hot pot dishes being passed among neighbours. Layers of meat, potatoes and onions are covered with suet pastry crust and baked in the oven, and, as with hot pot, the pie is served with pickled red cabbage, beetroot or onions.

Potato cakes can be bought in many shops and on market stalls, the average price today being 10p each (1988); cooked mashed potatoes, butter, flour and milk are made into small cakes and baked on a griddle or in a hot oven. They are best eaten hot for tea, generously buttered.

Fish and Chips first appeared in England in the second half of the nineteenth century. Lees of Mossley, a town on the outskirts of Manchester, claims to be the original fish and chip shop. In 1863 John Lees set up a wooden hut opposite the Stainford Arms to sell hot pigs' feet and pea soup. He added chipped potatoes to his menu after a visit to Oldham, where he probably met a tripe dresser called Dyson who in turn may have been the first to unite fish and chips. Fish and chips has continued to be a popular meal for dinner or tea, often eaten with 'mushy' peas, an adjective which aptly describes their consistency. Fish and chips are undoubtedly at their best eaten with the fingers from a paper wrapping, and many people say they have never tasted the same since newspaper went out and hygiene came in. Perhaps even better loved in Lancashire are *chip butties*, sandwiches of white bread lavishly spread with butter and filled with hot, well salted and vinegared chips, chips hot enough to melt the butter. The soggy consistency of pre-sliced white bread is essential in order to enjoy a chip buttie at its best. *Hot roast potatoes* were, until quite recently, widely available in markets. The name is a misnomer, as what you received for your penny was a greaseproof-paper bag full of tiny potatoes boiled in their jackets in a brass boiler looking not unlike Stephenson's Rocket. They can still be bought from a stall in the Guildhall Square, Preston.

Tripe and other offal

Another regional delicacy particularly associated with Lancashire is *tripe and onions*. Tripe shops were common until quite recently, usually UCP shops (United Cattle Products). Market stalls in towns such as Chorley, Bolton, Wigan and Bury still sell tripe, trotters, cow heel, weesum and elder. *Tripe* is the stomach of a cow dressed for sale by cleaning and boiling. The stomach is divided into four parts:

1. The rumen which gives seam or blanket tripe. The outer surface of the rumen is ridged into smooth seams (thick seams); the rest has a rougher texture (sometimes called blanket).
2. The reticulum which gives honeycomb tripe so called because of its characteristic appearance and considered by connoisseurs to be superior to seam.
3. The omasum, a continuation of the second stomach which gives a flimsy tripe no longer available (bible, monkshood, or psalterium).
4. The abomasum, the true digestive stomach, giving black, book, manifold manyplies or raggy tripe.

In addition the oesophagus or weesum is also eaten. Some stalls also sell pig's stomach which, as the pig is not a ruminant, only has one chamber resembling abomasum tripe. Tripe is eaten cold with salt and vinegar or cooked with milk and onions.

Cow heel is also sold on tripe stalls, being used alone or with steak in pies and stews to give a characteristic gelatinous quality to gravy. It can also be used to make cowheel brawn. *Sheeps' trotters* (in Lancashire 'trotters' always means sheeps' feet, not pigs' feet) are sold ready cooked either singly or in gangs of four. They are eaten stewed in milk, or battered and deep fried, or with oatmeal. Cooked with oatmeal they form a ceremonial part of the dinners of Bolton Wanderers Football Club, nickname the Trotters. The cooked trotters are cut up and oatmeal is used to thicken the stock in which the trotters were cooked. The meat is added to the thickened stock and the dish

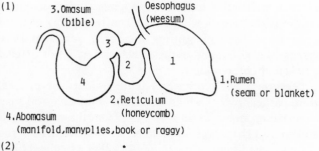

(1)

3.Omasum
(bible)

Oesophagus
(weesum)

1.Rumen
(seam or blanket)

2.Reticulum
(honeycomb)

4.Abomasum
(manifold,manyplies,book or raggy)

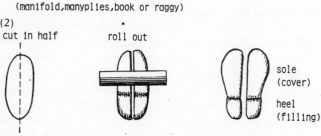

(2)

cut in half

roll out

sole
(cover)

heel
(filling)

18.
(1) Tripe: the
stomachs of the cow
and their names.
(2) How to make
Lancashire colliers
foots.

served with hot buttered toast. *Elder* is cooked cow's udder.[6] The raw udder is first drained of milk, and then boiled until tender. Elder can be bought pressed or unpressed, and is eaten alone with salt and vinegar, or sandwiched as a filling in barm cakes, or fried in butter. It has a taste reminiscent of tongue.

Separate from tripe stalls, cooked meat stalls are another feature of Lancashire markets. They display an enticing variety of goods; as well as the usual ham, tongue, beef, corned beef and pork, one can select from pressed beef, jellied beef, jellied chicken, cow heel, brawn, brisket, jellied lamb's tongues, roast ox heart, beef paste and salmon paste, the latter a great favourite for Sunday tea. The stalls also sell barm cakes, potato cakes and oatcakes, and many stall-holders will slice barm cakes and fill them with your choice of meat. Pies in profusion are also sold, small bridge or whist pies, pork pies in all sizes, meat and potato pies, cheese and onion pies, steak and kidney pies. Barbequed

Cooked meats

chicken stalls are a modern development, rows of spitted chickens rotating slowly round a central grilling element until done. Bags of stuffing measured out from large dishes can be bought at the same time as a hot or cold chicken or chicken joint.

Lancashire or Collier's foot (plural – foots, never feet) were pasties, two of which fitted into a miner's oval snap or snapping tin. The tin was hung from the miner's belt and an oval shape was found to be most convenient in the cramped conditions of the mine. A Collier's foot was filled with meat, onions and potatoes, a Lancashire foot contained cheese, onions and sometimes bacon. To make foots, shortcrust pastry is rolled out to form a thick oval. This is then cut in half lengthwise and each piece rolled out thinly from its centre to its end thereby enlarging it to form the sole. The filling is put on the thicker heel piece and the sole folded over to enclose it. When several are ready they are laid in a baking-tray, and the tray of foots is put to bake in the oven.

No one knows for certain how long *black puddings* have been made in Bury, nor why the town should be famous for this delicacy. Printed records show that the puddings have been made for sale in Bury since 1818; but it is likely that they were already being sold there in the middle ages. Casewell's shop, which was in Union Street, is recorded in the 1861 census as being occupied by Thomas Suthers, Black Pudding-maker and his wife Eliza, and there are tenuous links between Thomas Suthers and John or Anne Whitehead who were pudding makers according to the 1818 Directory. Mr Vincent Ashworth, the last owner of Casewell's shop before it was demolished in 1968, claims his recipe was the oldest known and has never been altered. The shop was most unusual. Through the window one could see the counter, a white marble slab on which stood a plateful of puddings and a set of scales. The other furniture in the room comprised a large bookcase containing a complete edition of Dickens, and a chiming clock on the mantelpiece. Each maker in Bury keeps his recipe secret, but all puddings contain fresh pig's blood, groats, cubes of pork fat and seasoning, including penny royal or pudding grass, and other herbs and spices. Cows' intestines are used as casings as sheeps' or pigs' are too tender. Thompsons (who can trace their recipe back to 1865) still sell puddings in Bury market. One can buy them raw to cook at home or hot from the stall's boiler, in which case the stallholder will split them in half and add a generous dab of mustard so they are ready to eat. By the end of the day the discarded skins are a hazard underfoot. It was impressed on well-brought-up children (such as myself) that to eat a hot pudding in the market was common, low and not done. In my youth in the 1940s puddings cost ninepence (3¾p) per pound weight. Today they retail at 74p. Most Lancastrians prefer boiled black puddings, but sometimes they are eaten sliced and fried with bacon.

Bacon ribs were popular for tea up to the 1950s. The ribs, removed by the grocer from a side of bacon before it was rolled for slicing, were boiled in a piece, then cut up and eaten with the fingers. The advent of plastic-packed ready-sliced bacon put an end to this delicacy.

Black or Carlin peas used to be sold at fairs and from street barrows. When vinegar is added to a bowl of peas, the cooking liquid turns milky, forming 'gutter slush'. According to legend, during a cotton famine a boat-load of peas arrived and saved the workers from starvation. The event was commemorated on Carlin Sunday, the Sunday before Palm Sunday.

Hindle Wakes or *Hen de la Wakes* has a long history, and could have its origins in a medieval dish. A boiled fowl is served cold surrounded by prunes and parsley. The breast of the bird is coated with white sauce and garnished with finely grated lemon zest. The dish is highly coloured, a feature of food of that period, and the use of lemon peel gives a similar effect to that of the medieval practice of endoring.

Lancashire cheese

Lancashire cheese, recognised by its white crumbly texture and clean mellow flavour, is still made in the traditional way on four farms and at five dairies around Preston. The cheese is made by an unusual method in which curds of two or three days' making are mixed together, giving the cheese its characteristic texture, colour and flavour. The cheese ripens early, being ready for consumption after one month; after this time it increases steadily in pungency and bite, and experts claim it is at its peak after three months. A young cheese can be spread easily with a knife, and any hint of acidity indicates an under-ripe cheese. Lancashire is said to be the best cheese in the world for cooking, as it does not separate out readily on heating. It is especially suitable for toasting, and in the past the best cheese was claimed to be made at Leigh and was nicknamed 'Leigh Toaster'.

To make the cheese, milk from the evening's milking is kept overnight and added to the morning's milking. A lactic acid starter is added and the milk is heated and allowed to ripen to develop the required level of acidity. Rennet is then added to form a junket which is cut by hand with cheese knives. This breaks the junket down into solid curds and liquid whey, and after the whey has been drained off the curds are left to develop the acidity. Unlike other cheeses, the curds are kept and curds of two or three days making are milled and blended together before salting and pressing. It is the mixing of curds which gives the cheese its characteristic qualities (whiteness and crumbly texture). The curds are then pressed in muslin-lined moulds for twenty-four hours to expel more whey, knocked out, and put in muslin binder sleeves with a muslin top and bottom cap. After further pressing for twenty-four hours, the cheeses are knocked out and allowed to dry before dipping in hot wax to seal them. They are then left to mature, most being sold after one month. The traditional method of sealing the outside with butter has been superseded by wax which is cleaner to handle, and in addition the cheese matures a little more quickly. The cheese is made in various sizes and each one is stamped with a number indicating the dairy or farm of origin. Sage cheese made by adding chopped sage to the curds is traditionally eaten at Christmas.

Lancashire cheese is excellent eaten with bread or oatcakes, or toasted. *Cheese and onion pies* are also made and a favourite dish is *cheese and onions*. Grated cheese is added to chopped onions previously boiled in a little milk and the mixture is then gently heated to melt the cheese before serving it with toast, barm cakes or oatcakes.

Morecambe Bay

Until the 1974 reorganisation of the county boundaries, Furness and much of Morecambe Bay was in Lancashire; now they are incorporated into Cumbria. It is an area quite distinct from the rest of Lancashire; apart from Barrow there is no industry, and the shipyard there is a relatively new development. The Bay itself is the dominant influence on the life of the people who live on its shores, a vast area of sand and scars deeply scored by the channels and dykes of the rivers and streams which flow into the bay. The sands are covered only at high tide and it can be treacherous for anyone who does not know them to venture out onto them without a guide.

The Bay yields many kinds of fish, fluke and shrimp the best known; but I have also eaten brill, dabs, plaice, dover sole, codling, garfish, smelts, sprats, whiting, whitebait, grey mullet, salmon, sea trout, eels, cockles, mussels and even on one memorable occasion a 5lb sea bass, taken from its waters. Flukes or flounders[7] are dextral flat fish which have given their name to the village of Flukeborough, many of whose inhabitants are still fishermen or employed by the local seafood industry. The fish come in with the tide to feed on the cockle beds. They are caught by nets, either a bawk net (a long net of a maximum of 150 yards set in a half-moon shape) or a stream or bag net (shaped like a V, the arms of the V being forty to fifty yards long and leading down to a bag). The net is set so the bag is in a dyke at low tide, ensuring the fish stay alive as the tide recedes. Locals also catch fish by feeling with their bare feet – a skilled operation in which I have never succeeded. Flukes freshly caught and fried in butter are not to be despised.

The cockles upon which the flukes feed also provide a source of income for fishermen, although hard back-breaking work to harvest. A wooden jumbo, resembling an upturned bench 4' 6" long with handles at each end, is rocked back and forth on the sand covering the cockle beds. This imitates the effect of the incoming tide and brings the cockles to the surface. They then have to be raked up by hand. Cockles can also be gathered using a three-legged stick called a cramb. Casts of sand on the surface show where the cockles are buried. The cramb is pushed in and the cockle picked up by hand. Cockles are sold locally, alive or boiled and picked out of their shells.

Morecambe Bay is probably best known for its *potted shrimps*. This way of preserving shrimps has been recorded since the eighteenth century. Originally a paste was made of butter, shrimps and spices. Now the shrimps are mixed with melted butter, mace and nutmeg, packed into small pots or cartons and covered with a layer of melted butter to seal them and exclude the air. Twenty years ago horses and carts were still used to catch shrimps, and I can remember watching the fishermen at work, the patient horses up to their withers in water in all weathers. Tractors have now replaced the horses. The tractor is hitched to a trailer carrying the net and riddles. On reaching the shrimping grounds the trailer is unhitched and the net attached, and as the tractor moves along the channel, steel bars on the base of the net mouth scrape the bottom of the channel. This disturbs the shrimps in the uppermost layer of sand, and as they jump up they are swept into the net. The catch is then riddled through a sieve to get rid of debris such as small crabs and broken shells. The shrimps must be boiled

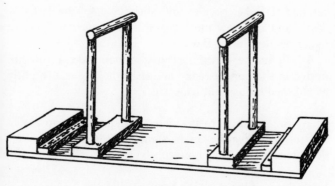

19.
A jumbo, used to bring cockles to the surface of the sands in Morecambe Bay.

in sea water whilst still alive; otherwise they are difficult to pick from the shells. Formerly the shrimps would be boiled and picked at home; now work is done by women who work in small co-operatives on piece-work rates. A skilled picker can pick 7 lb rough shrimps in one hour, yielding about 2 lb picked shrimps which retail at 50p for 2 oz. The pay (1988) was 74p a pound picked weight.

Cedric Robinson wrote:

> Another delicacy, which was only available at certain times of the year when shrimp fishing was in full swing, was made from the many small flukes caught with the shrimps. Instead of throwing them back they were brought home, their heads and tails snipped off with a pair of sharp scissors. Without any further cleaning, they were put into a stew-pot with alternate layers of butter and flukes. Then the pot, when filled to the top, was either put into a very slow old-fashioned fireside oven; or the dish was roasted. When ready, this delicacy could be cut up into sections, being served like a cake, and was greatly relished by the fishermen and their families.[8]

Sadly, pollution and overfishing have drastically reduced

catches of fluke, cockles and shrimps over the last few years, and in a few more years' time there could be no fishermen left in the Bay.

A little further down the coast, salmon and sea trout are netted in the Lune estuary, and fish-smoking is a recently established industry in Lancaster.

Sweet dishes Many sweet dishes are associated with particular towns.

Ormskirk gingerbread is mentioned in a song which dates back to the early nineteenth century.

> Ormskirk is a funny little town,
> And long ago 'twas said
> To be celebrated for old maids
> As well as gingerbread.

Chorley cakes, a plainer variation of Eccles cakes, are made from shortcrust pastry filled with currants. They are usually eaten spread with butter. *Currant Roger* is a local name given to a larger turnover made with similar ingredients. *Rossendale sad cakes* are yet another variation of pastry and currants. Sugar, suet, lard, flour, and currants are mixed together, formed into flat rounds and baked. Batches of sad cakes were taken with them when a family went away for the Wakes Week Holidays.[9]

Wet Nellie, a Liverpudlian dish, was originally a cheap way of using stale bread and crusts. These were crumbled and mixed with suet, sugar or syrup and a little spice before baking and cutting into pieces. The bottom piece of a pile was considered the best value for money as, hopefully, the syrup would have soaked through the other layers. 'Wet' probably refers to the sticky syrup, 'Nellie' being derived from Nelson. A similar dish is known as Nelson's cake or Nelson's slice in Plymouth, and in Norfolk where Nelson was born. All the recipes are variants of bread pudding, which could be eaten hot as a pudding or cold as cake. A modern recipe from Crosby, Merseyside, is much

20.
Shrimping with horse, cart and net in Morecambe Bay.

richer, using cake crumbs, raisins, lemon rind, milk and syrup to fill a pastry case.

Flat Mary Ann, a pudding from Ormskirk, is another variation of the old bread pudding. *Manchester pudding*, recorded in several mid and late nineteenth century cookery books,[10] is a variation of Queen of Puddings, and again uses breadcrumbs. *Wycoller cake*, also known as *love paste* or *courting cake*, can still be bought today. It comprises two layers of rich shortcrust pastry with a layer of jam spread between them before baking.

Other cakes, biscuits and pastries are associated with special days in the calendar. *Parkin* is eaten on bonfire night. Unlike Yorkshire parkin, Lancashire parkin contains more syrup and oatmeal and less flour. The parkin recipe I have given (p. 142) is one I found in my great Aunt Minnie's recipe book. *Eccles cakes* are associated with the Wakes holiday in September which begins on 1 September and lasts a further three days. During this time bull-baiting, cock-fighting and donkey races took place, as well as a fair and a fiddling match for the prize of a piece of silver. Puritans banned such festivities, along with the eating of rich cakes and spicy dried fruit pastries and pies, because of their religious significance, the spices which came from the East having connections with the gifts of the Magi.

The Act of 1650 which authorised the imprisonment of anyone eating or selling the forbidden cakes and pastries has never been repealed. The recipe is said to be a secret one of Elizabeth Raffald which she gave to a servant girl as a wedding present. The girl went to live in Eccles, and started to make and sell the cakes there.

Mrs Raffald, author of *The Experienced English Housekeeper* (1769), was housekeeper to the Warburtons of Arley Hall, Cheshire, and after her marriage ran a confectionery shop in Fennel Street, Manchester. Romantic though the story is, the cakes were being made at an earlier date. Mrs Raffald's book does not contain a recipe, but there is one in *Vegetable Cookery* by a member of the Bible Christian Church, which was published in 1829 in London and Manchester. The northern location perhaps explains the inclusion of the recipe, as it predates considerably any other named recipe I have been able to find in recipe books. The cakes are made with a spicy currant filling in a puff pastry case, although some early recipes mix all the ingredients together to form a stiff curranty dough which is rolled out thinly and cut into rounds. The cakes continued to be made in secret despite the 1650 Act, and in the nineteenth century two shops were renowned for them: Bradburns, the original shop, and Wardles for whom Bradburns made the cakes, as Wardles had no ovens. Bradburns was demolished in 1915 but Wardles still sells the cakes today.

The cakes are commemorated in the Eccles Wake Song

> When racing and fighting were all at an end,
> To ale-house each went with a sweet heart or friend;
> Some went to Shaw's, others Phillips chose,
> But me and my Moll to The Hare and Hounds goes.

> *Chorus*

> With music and cakes,
> For to keep up the Wakes,
> Among wenches and fine country beaux.

Sly cakes are similar small pastries filled with dried fruits.

Several traditional dishes are linked to Lent, Easter and Whitsuntide. *Fig pie* or *Fag pie* is still eaten in Blackburn. Opinions vary as to which is Fig Sunday. Some claim mid-Lent or Mothering Sunday, some the fifth or sixth Sunday in Lent. *Goosnargh cakes* can be bought at Goosnargh Post Office and in surrounding towns. It was estimated that at one time over 50,000 were sold during Whitsuntide at one shilling (5p) per dozen (they were 22p each in 1988). No one can agree on the origin of these distinctive biscuits which resemble a shortbread, flavoured with caraway and coriander and with a thick sugary crust.

Pace or *Pascal* eggs are rolled down a hill at Preston on Easter Monday. These are highly decorated hard-boiled eggs, and the aim is to get the egg to roll as far as possible without the shell breaking. Cracked eggs are forfeit to the owners of sound eggs.

Bury simnel

I have left until last Bury simnels,[11] as I have a connection with them. My great aunts Minnie and Maggie Pollard (1863–1945 and 1868–1929 respectively), sisters of my grandfather Henry Pollard, opened a confectioners' shop in Bury at the turn of the century. Minnie made the plainer cakes, and Maggie the fancy decorated ones. I have a manuscript recipe book of theirs which contains several recipes for simnels, some older than others. None of them, interestingly, include almond paste in the middle or on top although this is common practice today. Henry, who was at one time Superintendent of Bury Cemetery, made wooden boxes (possibly using coffin off-cuts?) in which cakes were posted to customers outside Bury. As the cakes were round and the boxes square, a black pudding was wedged in each corner to hold the cake in place. Despite the romantic story of Simon and Nellie who could not agree how to cook the cake, hence, simnel, the name is thought to derive from *simila*, a fine white flour used by the Romans to make bread or cake. Early simnels were a type of curranty spiced bread baked flat, not moulded in a tin. Gradually they became richer and more heavily fruited, resembling the moulded plum cakes of the eighteenth and nineteenth centuries. These cakes often used ale yeast or barm as a raising agent, and it is interesting to note one of Minnie's recipes is for barm simnel. The early simnels seem to have been boiled before they were baked, probably with a protective crust of flour paste. Many housewives sent goods to be baked at the local bakers as they lacked the facilities at home, and perhaps the fee charged for baking made it advisable to part-cook the cake at home first. Saffron, a popular yellow colouring, added to the paste would have given the cake a golden crust. This survives in the almond paste icing, and the almonds, once used in the cake mixture, now form a layer of almond paste in the middle. The almond paste balls, traditionally eleven in number, (representing the apostles except Judas) can be traced back to the shape of the early bread-like simnels. These were made in the form of a rounded centre with flatter edges which were rolled over and scalloped. Simnels are traditionally connected with Mothering Sunday, which may have evolved from the ancient Roman festival of Matronalia held on March 1st in honour of Juno. It used to be the custom to visit the mother church on Mothering Sunday and there would no doubt then have been a family reunion with special festive fare. Gradually this came to be the day when children who had left home would return to visit their parents, taking small tokens of their affection with them.

Herrick wrote about the custom in the early seventeenth century:

> I'll to thee a simnel bring
> 'Gainst though go'st a-mothering
> So that, when she blesseth thee
> Half that blessing thou'lt give me.

The Bury simnel is attributed to Lydia Hutchinson, née Holt, and her daughter Mary, who were the only professed pastry cooks and confectioners in Bury 'and gave great celebrity to the Bury Simnel'.[12]

People travelled up to forty miles to buy the simnels on Mothering Sunday, and they would no doubt refresh themselves before returning. Contemporary writers in the early nineteenth century reported that the town was like a fair with confectioners' shops open all day for the sale of cakes, and ale-houses for the sale of bragot, a kind of spiced ale. In the middle of the nineteenth century, Bury's clergy united in an attempt to stop the disorderly scenes; but it was not until the licensing laws of 1871 restricted opening on Sundays from 1 pm–3 pm and 7 pm–9 pm that revelry and drunken disorder on that day came to an end.

The earliest recorded recipe dates from 1870 and is for a richly fruited, yeast raised cake not baked in a tin. Florence White in *Good Things in England*[13] gives a recipe contributed by a Mrs Huggins, which Mrs Huggins claims is the recipe for the original cake; and it is similar to the 1780 recipe except that it uses sal volatile (ammonium carbonate) as a raising agent. I tried the recipe, noting in passing the remarkable amount of spice in the cake (1 oz to 2½ lb flour). The reason for this becomes clear on testing. Sal volatile decomposes on heating to produce ammonia, and even this amount of spicing failed to mask the unpleasant taste. Mrs Hutchinson's descendants continued as confectioners well into the nineteenth century, and a descendant opened up a shop in Princes Street which was still selling simnels up to its demolition in 1968.

Lancashire, then, is a county of contrasts – in scenery, land, work and food. Sadly, many of the region's food specialities are no longer available and exist only in books; but some can still be found, especially in the homes and on the bustling markets of the cotton towns. How long this will be so, in the face of competition from takeaways, burger bars and kebab houses, is hard to say, as it is mainly the older generation who buy and cook traditional foods. However, perhaps all is not lost: I noticed that my local freezer shop lists mushy peas and hot pot among its products, and cans of tripe and onions have been reported to be stocked in Harrods.

Notes and References

1. Sir J. P. Kay Shuttleworth, *The Moral and Physical Conditions of the Working Classes Employed in the Cotton Manufacture in Manchester*, 2nd ed. (London, 1832).

2. See, for example, Friedrich Engels, *The Condition of the Working Classes in England (1845)* translated by W. O. Henderson and W. H. Chaloner (Oxford, 1958), p. 10; Christopher Aspin, *Lancashire, the First Industrial Society* (Helmshore Local History Society, 1969), p. 44f.

3. *Leaves from Gerard's Herbal (1597)* arranged by Marcus Woodward (Oxford, 1927), p. 217.

4. R. N. Salaman, *The History and Social Influence of the Potato* [corrected ed.] (Cambridge, 1985), p. 453.

5. E. Hyams, *English Cottage Gardens* (Harmondsworth, Penguin, 1970), p. 57.

6. For a more detailed study, see Lynda Brown, 'Elder: "A Good Udder to Dinner".' *Petits Propos Culinaires* 26 (1987), pp. 60–4.

7. 'Maximum length about 50 cm. This is a dextral fish, but reversed examples are common. The eyed side is dull brown, greyish or dull green. It may bear orange speckles (not as bright as the orange spots of the plaice). The blind side is dead white . . . The flounder, which ranges from the Mediterranean to the White Sea is common in estuaries and especially abundant in the Baltic Sea. It is much more important as a food fish in northern Europe than in Britain. Its own diet features bivalves. It likes to come in with the tide and browse on cockle beds during the period of high tide . . . The flounder is inferior to the plaice and has even been condemned as "watery, poor eating". At its worst it may be, but its quality varies and a good flounder is not at all to be despised. Fry or steam'. Alan Davidson, *North Atlantic Seafood* (London, 1979), p. 149.

8. C. Robinson, *One Man's Morecambe Bay* (Clapham, Dalesman, 1984), p. 29. Cedric Robinson is Guide to the Sands as well as a fisherman working the bay for fluke, shrimps and cockles. As Guide he has an intimate knowledge of the bay and its dangerous sands.

9. A wake was originally an all-night vigil or watch in church on the eve of the anniversary of the dedication of the church. Wakes spilled over into the churchyards, becoming rowdy, drunken celebrations. Eventually they became fairs, and the name has continued in Lancashire to mean the annual local holidays, when the mills and most of the other businesses and shops in a town

shut for a week. There was a mass exodus of people from the towns, off to stay in seaside boarding houses. It was customary for them to provide the food for the landlady to cook, a practice which continued up to the 1930s. Blackpool was the most popular holiday resort, followed by Morecambe and Southport.

10. See, for example, *Cassells Dictionary of Cookery* (London, c.1890); I. Beeton, *Book of Household Management* (London, 1861).
11. For a more detailed study see C. Anne Wilson, 'I'll to Thee a Simnel Bring', *Petits Propos Culinaires 19* (1985), p. 46.
12. B. T. Barton, *History of the Borough of Bury* (Bury, 1876).
13. Florence White, *Good Things in England* (London, 1932), p. 333.
14. Mary Norwak *Cakes* (London, 1984), p. 146; Lizzie Boyd, *ed.*, *British Cookery* (London, 1976); recipe given to me by Mrs Joyce Taylor, from her mother (born 1900) who was a confectioner in Chorley.

Recipes

Simnel Cake, 1780

5 lb plain flour	½ lb finely cut almonds
4 lb currants	½ oz nutmeg
1 lb raisins	10 eggs
½ lb candied peel	¼ pint cream
1 lb sugar	¾ pint barm
1 to 2 lb butter	

Make into cakes using 4 lb to 6 lb mixture. (Too much butter makes it difficult for the knobs of scalloped edge to keep in shape)

Great Aunt Minnie's Barm Simnel

2½ lb plain flour	¼ lb shredded almonds
2½ lb currants	¼ oz cinnamon
1½ lb raisins	3 nutmegs
¼ lb candied peel	4 eggs
1½ lb sugar	⅓ pint milk
½ lb lard	1 oz bicarbonate of soda
¾ lb butter	1 oz barm (yeast)

3 x 8" rounds – 2 to 2½ hours very slow [oven].

Bury Simnel (traditional)

1 lb plain flour	½ tsp nutmeg
9 oz currants	½ tsp cinnamon
8 oz raisins	4 eggs
2 oz candied peel	4 tabsp milk
8 oz sugar	2 tsp baking powder
9 oz butter	

2 x 6" rounds. Moderate oven, 25 minutes.

Simnel (Florence White)[13]

2½ lb plain flour	¾ lb shredded almonds
4 lb currants	½ oz nutmeg
½ lb candied peel	5 eggs
1½ lb sugar	1 oz cinnamon
½ lb lard	1 oz salts of ammonia
¾ lb butter	

Batch loaf 18" across, 2½" to 3" deep. Slow oven, 1½ to 2 hours.

Goosnargh cakes[14]

6 oz flour	½ tsp caraway seeds
4 oz butter	½ tsp ground coriander
1 oz sugar	extra sugar for sprinkling

1. Mix first five ingredients together.
2. Roll ⅜" deep and cut into 2" rounds.
3. Sprinkle over ¼" layer of sugar.
4. Leave for six hours to twelve hours.
5. Bake on greased sheets 30 to 40 minutes until pale but firm at 140°C gas mark 1.

Chorley cakes (Family Recipe)

8 oz short crust pastry made with lard
4 oz currants

1. Roll the pastry out ¼" thick. Cut into 6" rounds.
2. Divide currants between rounds. Moisten edges and bring together. Roll out until currants show through.
3. Bake for 15 to 20 minutes at 400°F (200°C), gas mark 6.

Lancashire Parkin (Great Aunt Minnie)

8 oz oatmeal	2 oz brown sugar
3 oz plain flour	4 oz lard
1 level tsp ginger	8 oz treacle and syrup mixed
½ oz bicarbonate of soda	2½ fl. oz milk

1. Melt sugar, lard, treacle and syrup over low heat.
2. Mix oatmeal, flour, and ginger in a bowl.
3. Add the cooled melted mixture.
4. Add the bicarbonate of soda mixed in the milk.
5. Mix and divide between 2 x 7" tins lined and greased.
6. Bake for 1½ hours 300°F (150°C), gas mark 2.

142

6.

Prodigal Frugality:
Yorkshire Pudding and Parkin,
Two Traditional Yorkshire Foods

JENNIFER STEAD

In the early years of Queen Victoria's reign, the English national dish, which for at least a century and a half had been roast beef and plum pudding, became roast beef and Yorkshire pudding. Why should Yorkshire pudding, a regional dish, be adopted as a national one? It must be that by this time, in the national imagination, it had ousted plum pudding as the starchy accompaniment to meat (though plum pudding lingered on in the first course for another fifty years).[1] What is the character of Yorkshire pudding, that it should achieve such prominence, and how and when did Yorkshire pudding originate?

Yorkshire pudding

Yorkshire pudding must have been in existence for some time before its first mention in print. A pancake batter (which is what Yorkshire pudding is made of) had been used for centuries, fried as pancakes or fritters; in the seventeenth century it was boiled in pudding cloths and in the eighteenth century also baked in the oven.[2] But at some point in the late seventeenth or early eighteenth century this batter was poured into a greased hot pan, cooked on the bottom a little, then placed under meat that was roasting on a spit before the fire, where it finished cooking and was flavoured with the fat and juices dripping onto it. The first printed reference to this so far discovered, appeared in 1737 in a large anonymous compendium recipe book called *The Whole Duty of a Woman*, and the recipe, called 'A Dripping Pudding', runs:

143

Make a good batter as for pancakes, put it in a *hot* toss-pan over the fire with a bit of butter to fry the bottom a little, then put the pan and butter under a shoulder of mutton, instead of a dripping pan, keeping frequently shaking it by the handle and it will be *light* and savoury, and fit to take up when your mutton is enough, then *turn* it on a dish and serve it *hot*. [My italics.]

Since the author of *The Whole Duty of a Woman* (the evidence points to that author being a man) is merely a compiler of recipes stolen from other authors, rather than a cook, it seems probable that 'A Dripping Pudding' originated somewhere else, in another printed cookery book or manuscript which has not survived. This recipe is simply a large over-thick pancake made in the usual pancake pan, which was the toss-pan or frying pan. It is started off on the fire, as a pancake would be made, and was just finished off under roasting meat. (The juices dripping from roasting meat were used especially at Feast and holiday times, when even the less well-off roasted a piece of beef and they placed bits of oatcake, or bread or pieces of boiled pudding in the dripping tin to make 'sops'.) The recipe stresses that the batter should be poured in a *hot* pan; the shaking implies a crusty bottom that will slide about; 'it will be *light*'; it should be turned upside down when the crusty bottom will be uppermost; and it must be served *hot*, implying it is to be eaten immediately. All these points, apart from the shaking, apply to the truly successful Yorkshire pudding.

The next mention in print of a pudding cooked under meat in this way is by Hannah Glasse, in her famous and influential *The Art of Cookery Made Plain and Easy*, 1747. Hannah Glasse copied and adapted no less than 264 recipes from *The Whole Duty of a Woman* and its re-issue as *The Lady's Companion* 1740, and she could have tried the recipe and 'improved' it. However, the fact that Hannah

Glasse called the recipe 'A Yorkshire Pudding' – apparently the first writer to do so – implies that she had further knowledge of it, gleaned perhaps from another printed source, or from a friend or a cook. As she says, 'it is an exceeding good pudding'.[3] Here it is:

A Yorkshire Pudding

Take a Quart of Milk, four Eggs, and a little Salt, make it up into a thick Batter with Flour, like a Pancake Batter. You must have a good Piece of Meat at the Fire, take a Stew-pan and put some Dripping in, set it on the Fire, when it boils, pour in your Pudding, let it bake on the fire till you think it is nigh enough, then turn a Plate upside-down in the Dripping-pan, that the Dripping may not be blacked; set your Stew-pan on it under your Meat, and let the Dripping drop on the Pudding, and the Heat of the Fire come to it, to make it of a fine brown. When your Meat is done and set to Table, drain all the Fat from your Pudding, and set it on the Fire again to dry a little; then slide it as dry as you can into a Dish, melt some Butter, and pour into a Cup, and set in the Middle of the Pudding. It is an exceeding good Pudding, the Gravy of the Meat eats well with it.

Hannah Glasse has changed toss-pan to stew-pan, butter to dripping. Hers must be a deeper pudding, and in a stew-pan, impossible to shake and therefore, being undisturbed, likely to rise higher. It is cooked on the fire till almost done, then put under the meat. She stresses the fat in the pan must be boiling before the batter is poured in – a vital point in making true puffy Yorkshire pudding. The brown top would also be crisp. Though they appear to be from different sources, the two recipes are in essence the same, both point to a northern origin, and I would argue, most probably a Yorkshire one.[4]

Many dishes which have come to be attached to one

region were once much more universal, and the thrusting of a cooking pancake under roasting meat or the baking of pancake batter in a stew-pan under roasting meat could have been widespread in early eighteenth century England. However, there are a few slender clues in the afore-mentioned recipes which point to their being of north country origin, for example, the roasting shoulder of mutton (beef was the most popular meat in England as a whole) and the fact that Hannah Glasse's family was northern. In visiting relatives in Northumberland her route from London would have been up and down the busy Great North Road, with its numerous inns, where the constant roasting of large joints of meat for travellers and other patrons was facilitated, especially in the north, by plentiful supplies of cheap coal. Hannah Glasse could have got her recipe from one of these inns in Yorkshire and so called it 'Yorkshire' pudding. Because her recipe book was immensely popular – it went into seventeen editions between 1747 and 1803 – and hugely plagiarised, it must have played a large part in the popularisation of Yorkshire pudding. That this pudding was served at Yorkshire inns is certain: the Hon. John Byng ate it with roast mutton and other dishes in 1792 at the White Swan, Middleham near Richmond, ('a better dinner, and better dress'd I have never sat down to').[5] Its economy is very Yorkshire in character. Although a first course of starchy 'padding' in the form of boiled puddings and dumplings was usual in many parts of England to prevent the eating of too much meat, a Yorkshire pudding is tarred with the brush of the county character. Yorkshiremen were notorious for their sharp practices, and for centuries, to 'have the Yorkshire put on you' or to suffer the 'Yorkshire bite' was to be cheated. At the same time, Yorkshire hospitality was fabled. So Yorkshire pudding is a triumphal marriage of those conflicting aspects of the Yorkshire character – meanness and liberality. It is cheap and hugely filling. In Yorkshire it was always, and still is, to be eaten on its own as a first course, cut into very large squares, with good gravy. There is also economy of effort – it saves one fiddling about with a pudding cloth or boiling water specially for the pudding.[6] When roasting meat, why not simply roast the pudding too?

If it cannot be documented that Yorkshire specifically originated the Yorkshire pudding, it can certainly be seen from recipes and other sources from the mid-eighteenth century that Yorkshire developed this pudding to a fine art. These sources reveal that the essence of a Yorkshire pudding is lightness and crispness, and that anything heavy and soggy is not a Yorkshire pudding but a mere batter pudding. Hannah Glasse's pudding must have been somewhat thicker than the later ideal one, but still light, tender and crisp. In 1769 the very practical and sensible Mrs Elizabeth Raffald published in Manchester *The Experienced English Housekeeper*, in which she instructs one to cut the cooked pudding into squares and to turn these over to brown the underside (still common practice in Yorkshire today) which implies this also was a light pudding, as a thick soggy one would be difficult to brown. This cutting into squares and turning is copied in the 1784 (posthumous) edition of Hannah Glasse, and thereafter by most writers. It is amusing to trace in countless printed Yorkshire pudding recipes for the next hundred or more years elements stolen from either Hannah Glasse or Mrs Raffald, and it is clear that some writers had never clapped eyes on, let alone cooked, a Yorkshire pudding. Some totally misunderstood the method, for they stir the batter in the pan on the fire, thereby making a kind of hasty pudding or custard; a recipe of 1804 instructs one to keep stirring until cool, then pour in the tin under the meat; another (1806) says the batter is 'to be poured into a saucepan, and stirred over the fire until cooked' when the saucepan was to be placed under the meat upon a plate (this last instruction stolen from the early Hannah Glasse). Some writers add nutmeg, ginger, even candied peel or currants.[7] Other non-northern writers do not seem familiar with the genuine article. Even *Beeton's Dictionary of Everyday Cookery* (1865) does not require the use of fierce heat, has the pudding cooked in the oven one hour before putting it under the meat, and then cut into *small* square pieces. The recipe in *Mrs A. B. Marshall's Cookery Book* (1887) is better, but commits the further heresy of adding baking powder (!) and cutting the pudding into 2" pieces, which to a Yorkshire person is absurd. All these books, but particularly the two last-mentioned very popular and influential ones may be partly responsible for the dismal failure of southern cooks up to the present day to make Yorkshire pudding.

Yorkshire visitors to the south are constantly disappointed. J. B. Priestley's Mr Oakroyd in *The Good Companions* (1929) searches his plate in vain for the Yorkshire pudding which his southern landlady declares is there. 'What!' says Mr Oakroyd, 'You don't mean this bit o' custard, soft batter stuff, under t' cabbage?' He instructs her about how to make it properly – the fierce heat necessary, the eating of it on its own, immediately it comes out of the oven, otherwise 'you might as well go and sole your boots with it'; it should be as light as a feather, 'crisp and brarn, just a top and a bottom, . . . wi' none o' this custardy stuff in t'middle.' Such judgements proliferate: 'In London and elsewhere I have invariably found it very thick resembling what we call in Yorkshire a batter pudding'.[8] Outside the county, the pudding still is, too often, solid flaccid slabs, flat and heavy, called by some Yorkshire women 'Hampshire puddings'.[9]

But could not these southern puddings have originated at the same time as Yorkshire pudding, and simply been a different regional version of the same thing? For example, the diaries of Thomas Turner, a shopkeeper in the village of East Hoathly, Sussex, reveal that in a very short period, a matter of ten months in 1757–8, he has batter pudding done under the meat several times.[10] He never calls it Yorkshire pudding. Outside this ten month period (at least in the published version of his diaries, only one third of which are printed) there is no more mention of it. Only a search of the complete diaries would reveal whether he eats batter pudding outside of this ten month period, or whether it was a passing fad; also whether the cook was a local person. The entries in the published *Diary* seem to suggest that his batter puddings are cooked by two means (if his use of the words *roasting* and *baking* are precise):

1.   under the meat which is *roasting* before the fire in a Dutch oven, or

2.   under the meat which is *baking* inside a brick oven.

Here are the entries: On the 23rd March 1756/7 his visitor was Molly French and they dined on 'fillet of leg of veal *roasted* in oven, with a pudding under it' (implying the Dutch oven or metal screen or hastener). A week later Mr Ralfe the sadler visits, and they have 'spare rib, *baked* in oven with a pudding under it', implying the brick oven. On the 14th July 1757 he has 'stuffed bullocks heart *baked* in oven with a pudding under it' implying brick oven; also in July, with his brother James Marchant's man, a 'loin mutton *roasted* in oven with a *plain* batter pudding under it'. On Christmas Day 1756 he has two visitors; dinner is 'sirloin of beef *roasted* in the oven with a batter pudding under it' etc. His use of the words roasted/baked may be arbitrary, in which case my theory of Dutch oven versus brick oven founders, but the kinds of meats cooked seem to support it: joints are roasted, less important cuts are baked. The baked spare rib and stuffed bullock's heart could have had the batter poured directly into the baking tin under and around the meat. He does have sausages done this way, and also plums in batter.[11] Thomas Turner does seem to have his batter pudding on rather special occasions, when entertaining visitors, or at Christmas, as a change from his usual boiled puddings.

Many non-Yorkshire people who make their pudding heavy and dense still call their pudding 'batter pudding' and not 'Yorkshire pudding'. May they not be correct? Are they not merely continuing their own region's tradition? May not the adoption of the Yorkshire type as the national dish have confusedly and unfairly applied the term 'Yorkshire' to all baked batter puddings, whatever their origin? So a soggy batter pudding, that never intended to be a Yorkshire one, is judged harshly. What does seem clear is that Yorkshire people did invent a special lightness and crispness. This accords with their fabled brusque temperaments: the fact that they require spanking hot fat, explosions as the batter hits it, fierce heat, and crisp results, may explain why it has often been said that only Yorkshire folk – those possessing the Yorkshire temperament – can make a true Yorkshire pudding. This same temperaments: the fact that they require spanking hot origin, in that boiled puddings are soft, pappy mush, and don't offer enough resistance to the teeth, whereas the crispness of Yorkshire pudding offers agreeable sensations to strenuous Yorkshire jaws (which may also explain why flour parkin was never as popular as oatmeal parkin and plain porridge not so esteemed as the more chewy 'lumpydicks').[12]

Very few people today can have tasted a real Yorkshire pudding, that is one done under meat roasting before a fire. At what point did it cease to be done under the meat? Mrs Catherine Buckton, Chairman of the Leeds Education Committee in 1882 and originator of the *Cookery Scheme of the Leeds School Board for the New Code 1882*, designed to instruct children of the working classes, in her lesson on Yorkshire pudding writes: 'A Yorkshire pudding is *always* placed under the meat to receive some of the dripping'. However, in the next twenty years the roasting of meat in front of the fire gave way to the method of 'roasting' or rather baking it in the oven, where, because of the bottom heat of a fire-oven the pudding could still be placed under the meat.[13] Early gas ovens were supplied with hooks in the top to hang the meat from, but it was found unsuccessful to put a pudding under it because the lower part of a gas oven is the coolest part, and a pudding requires the highest heat. After this time all sorts of hybrids abound in the pages of cookery books, for example, puddings cooked before the open fire but not under meat, or started in the oven and finished off under fire-roasting meat, or poured into the oven-tin in which meat is baking, or poured in the tin after the meat has been taken out; and confusions abound as to what authenticates the true Yorkshire pudding – some saying to be Yorkshire it *must* be done before the fire, others saying it *must* be done under the meat, and anything else is a mere batter pudding. By the turn of this century, on the whole, only institutions like inns and hotels, restaurants and clubs could afford to roast large joints of meat in the old-fashioned wasteful way (only the best quality meat could be used, and it shrank, and used enormous amounts of coal) and would therefore have been able to make a 'proper' Yorkshire pudding. Cast-iron fireside ovens were still plentiful until the 1940s and 50s and so in theory it was possible to continue baking a pudding under meat 'roasting' on the shelf above, or supported on a trivet in the same pan. But it is clear that Yorkshire pudding had been cooked on its own in the oven well before 1903 when the Leeds publication *Practical Cookery* by Amy Atkinson and Grace Holroyd gave this succinct instruction: 'Heat a little dripping in a tin, pour in the batter (it should be about ¼ inch in depth) and bake about 20 minutes in a quick oven. Cut in squares, and serve with gravy'. Since this is done neither in front of the fire, nor under meat, it is technically a batter pudding, but it is obvious that the term 'Yorkshire' is now attached to this impoverished kind; and it is in this impoverished form that we eat it today. It is however, still puffy and crisp, as the original was intended to be.

The greatest number of Yorkshire puddings per capita are probably still eaten in Yorkshire, but the greatest number per capita over the years must surely have been eaten by Yorkshire miners. Miners traditionally enjoyed the best food of all industrial workers, being able to afford meat every day; their wives made Yorkshire pudding practically every day too, often at midnight when the husband had been on a late shift. On Sundays in all the pit villages as the miners strolled home from the pub, 'the streets of tiny cottages were alive with the sound of carving knives being sharpened in unison – and clanging stove doors as the sizzling joints were lifted from their pans to make way for the Yorkshire pudding batter to be poured into the dripping'.[14] Until the 1950s, Yorkshire pudding featured in almost every Yorkshire household's Sunday dinner, as well as appearing at least once during the week.

Every cook has his or her own recipe; the proportions of plain flour to egg and liquid vary. The lightest batter is made with half milk and half water, as all milk cuts down the crispness; and to reduce the fat, skim or 'blue' milk was often used, or a handful of snow. In summer, one cup of beestings could be used in the place of two eggs. Some beat the batter before an open window 'to get more air in', some use a spoon, others a whisk. Some add a little cold water, others an eggcupful of boiling water at the last minute; some let the batter stand, others do not. Some cut and turn the pudding to crisp the bottom even more, others do not. A hot tin, boiling fat and hot oven are essential, as are diners already sitting round the table, knives and forks poised.[15] The pudding should be cut into large squares that cover the centre of a dinner plate, and served on its own with gravy before the meat and vegetables (this is observed in County Durham also). The accompaniments to Yorkshire pudding are legion, dictated by individual or family tastes. Our family ate it with sugar and gravy (we have dropped the sugar); others ate it with sugar and butter; some have mint sauce if lamb is to follow, or apple or parsley sauce if pork or ham are to follow. It can be eaten with onion gravy, raspberry or blackberry vinegar, relishes such as 'wet salad' or 'choppy' (salad stuff and fresh mint chopped up with sugar and vinegar), a mixture of jam and vinegar, or mustard, sugar and vinegar, or just golden syrup; but whatever the accompaniment, in Yorkshire it is always eaten before the meat.

In Lancashire it is also eaten as a dessert with custard or white sauce flavoured with rum, or with condensed milk, and in Northumberland with strawberries and cream. The batter is extremely adaptable and all kinds of additions can be sliced or sprinkled into it before it is popped in the oven (though when this is done it is no longer a classic Yorkshire pudding). Some of these are minced meat, sliced, raw onions or chopped, cooked onions or the whites of leeks, grated cheese, chopped rhubarb, sliced cooking apples and currants. The currant version was eaten with gravy, or sweet white sauce, before the meat.[16]

In the spirit of commercialised 'heritage', in 1989 Yorkshire pudding entered a new phase. In a series of fast food outlets, Grandma Batty's Traditional Yorkshire Pudding Emporia, frozen microwaved puddings cooked in vegetable oil and the size and shape of a dog's bowl, are now being sold with fillings such as vegetable curry, chilli con carne, burgers, sweetcorn, maple syrup and ice-cream, so that unsuspecting foreign visitors will think this stuff is genuine, traditional Yorkshire food. However, given the already strange accompaniments eaten with their pudding for so long by Yorkshire folk, they may even adopt these outlandish ones themselves. The commercial world (among other forces) has invented and is inventing new traditions all the time.

This is my mother's recipe (serves 2):

2 rounded tbs plain flour
1 egg
pinch salt
¼ pint mixed milk and water

The oven must be pre-heated to gas mark 8 or 9, 450–475°F (230–240°C). Sift the flour and salt, make a hole in the flour and drop the egg in with a little of the liquid and, using a fork, incorporate the flour, adding liquid by degrees, so that there are no lumps. Heat a 9"x9" tin with about 1 ounce of lard or dripping in a very hot oven till smoking hot. Keep it spanking hot on the burner while you pour the batter in (it should splutter), and immediately put in the top part of the oven. Bake at gas mark 8 for 20–25 minutes. Do not peep until after 20 minutes. Eat at once. (On the top shelf it may burn. If you smell burning, turn the heat down one notch. On the second shelf from the top you may need to keep the heat at its very hottest, gas mark 9, 475°F (240°C). Ovens differ and you may have to experiment.)

One rounded tablespoon of flour equals one ounce. A more luxurious pudding is made by using one tablespoon of flour to one small egg for each person. Mrs Raffald, in *The Experienced English House-keeper* (1769), was the first cookery writer I have found to use these proportions; she uses four (large eighteenth-century) tablespoons of flour and four eggs to three (wine) pints of milk (forty-eight English fluid ounces).

Elizabeth Raffald was, after Hannah Glasse, the most famous cookery writer of the eighteenth century. She was from a Doncaster family and her recipe suggests that even before 1769 Yorkshire pudding was being made from a thinner, lighter batter. Hannah Glasse (1747) had used only two (wine) pints of milk to four eggs, thus producing a thicker batter. Hannah Glasse's 1784 (posthumous) edition changes her old recipe by adding an extra egg, plus nutmeg and ginger (the ginger appears to have been stolen from Charlotte Mason's *The Ladies Assistant c.* 1780), and copying the cooking instructions from Mrs Raffald.

Other proportions, well tried and tested are:

3 tbs plain flour	4 tbs plain flour
1 or 2 eggs	1 or 2 large eggs
pinch salt	½ tsp salt
nearly ½ pint mixed milk	½ pint mixed milk
and water	and water

(This requires a tin about 11"x11", and 1½ ounces of fat.) Bake at gas mark 8, 450°F (230°C) for 25–30 minutes.

Notes and References

1. Meg Dods (Mrs Christobel Johnstone), *The Cook and Housewife's Manual* 6th edn. 1837, p. 341: 'this is the favourite English accompaniment to a sirloin of beef, or a loin of veal or mutton.' Plum pudding was still eaten with meat in the 1880s by the working class, cf. Catherine Buckton, *Cookery Scheme of the Leeds School Board for the New Code* (Leeds, 1882), p. 42.
2. For example: Thomas Tryon, *The Good Housewife made a Doctor* (1692), ix 75, 'In puddens it is usual to mix Flour, Eggs, Milk etc.' Puddings began to proliferate in the later seventeenth century to replace the now unfashionable pottages. Regions developed their own puddings according to available ingredients, fuel etc.
3. For an examination of Hannah Glasse's recipe sources and her innovations, see Jennifer Stead, 'Quizzing Glasse: or Hannah Scrutinized', *Petits Propos Culinaires* 13, pp. 9–24, and 14, pp. 17–30; and Priscilla Bain, 'Recounting the Chickens: Hannah further scrutinized', *PPC* 23, pp. 38–41.
4. I have not tried these recipes as it is difficult to reconstruct them; flour had a greater moisture content and was less fine than ours, eggs were smaller; it should also be remembered that the pint was smaller, being a wine pint (only 5/6 of an Imperial pint) and that the preliminary cooking of the pudding was done on the coals of a red-hot roasting fire which would give terrific all-round heat impossible to reproduce today except by the same means.
5. Hon. J. Byng, *Torrington Diaries* (London, 1936), vol. 3, p. 57. Yorkshire pudding also formed a regular part of the weekly menu in houses of the rich, for example, on Tyneside, at Seaton Delaval, a typical week's menu (August 29–September 6, 1789) in the Household Book (Newcastle Record Office 2-DE 30/3) shows that although other puddings appear with meats in the second course and on the sideboard, the only pudding to appear in the first course is Yorkshire pudding, which appears on two days, once with roast mutton and once with roast veal; on the two days they have roast beef, plum pudding is both times served with it in the old way. Menu quoted in Margaret Slack, *Northumbrian Fare* (Newcastle-Upon-Tyne, 1981), pp. 18–19.
6. The very popular 'plain puddings' were the same pancake batter boiled in a cloth 'in fair water' i.e. separately from the boiling meat. Coarser puddings could be boiled with the meat.
7. Leeds Mercury Supplement 18 July 1885, Local Notes and Queries.
8. Dupuis Brown, describing how a real Yorkshire pudding is made, in the early twentieth century writes 'The local preparation of Yorkshire pudding seems to have been quite a speciality, and I have never seen a faithful representation of it elsewhere', in

Florence White Good Things in England (reprinted London, 1968), p. 197.

9. Carol Wright, *Cassell's Country Cookbooks, Yorkshire* (London, 1975), p. 9.

10. T. Turner, *The Diary of Thomas Turner 1754-1765*, ed. D. Vasey (Oxford, 1984).

11. Bullock's heart could be roasted, cf. *The Diary of a Country Parson: The Revd. J. Woodforde 1758-1781*, ed. by John Beresford, Oxford University Press, 1926, Vol. 5 (1799) p. 111. In Norfolk the baking of meat in batter was called 'pudding pie' (OED). In Wales the batter was sweetened and baked with sultanas added in a pastry-lined dish, and was called pancake pudding (S. Minwel Tibbott, *Welsh Fare*, National Museum of Wales, 1976, p. 62).

12. For the nature of Yorkshire eating, see D. Elliston Allen, *British Tastes* (London, 1968).

13. 'We now roast in the oven more often than before the fire', *Mrs Beeton's All About Cookery* New ed. (London, 1909), p. 17.

14. The Guardian, 5 December 1987.

15. It is impossible to make Yorkshire pudding in a fan-assisted oven.

16. *Mrs Beeton's All About Cookery* (1909), p. 562; Peter Brears, *Traditional Food in Yorkshire* (Edinburgh, 1987), pp. 121-22; Peggy Hutchinson, *Old English Cookery* revised edn. (London, 1973), pp. 38-9; Yorkshire Women's Institute Recipe Book, *Through Yorkshire's Kitchen Door* (York, 1957), pp. 70-1; Dorothy Drake, *Laughter in the Kitchen* (London, 1979), pp. 7-9; Sheila Hutchins, *Grannie's Kitchen* (London, 1979), pp. 33-5; Shirley Kaye (ed.) *Yorkshire Cooking* (Halifax Courier, no date) p. 164; other recipes from personal communications.

In many parts of the north of England, no Guy Fawkes Night is considered complete without slabs of parkin made of oatmeal, treacle, butter and ginger. It is still eaten in some of these areas all year round, cooked usually as a large cake in a big, square Yorkshire pudding tin, or in biscuit form. In other areas it is made only in biscuit form. As I write (three weeks before November 5th) my local Huddersfield supermarket is offering to all shoppers who spend over £10 a free 500 gm bag of oatmeal and a free 2 lb tin of golden syrup, thereby illustrating that it is in those places where oats were once the staple grain that parkin-eating remains a very strong tradition; and that it remains especially strong in those small towns and villages where home-baking is still vigorous. It is the sort of cake one eats by the fistful, in hunks, though the biscuit variety is slightly daintier. Why does it come in these two varieties? The origins of parkin have never been fully explained, and the origin of its special relationship with November 5th has only been hinted at. I shall attempt to explore both.

Parkin, Tharf Cake and November 5th

Modern parkin is made with treacle and therefore is not likely to be older than the mid-seventeenth century. Molasses (from *mel*, meaning honey) came to be named treacle because it was used in the place of honey for mixing with drugs into a medicine called theriaca, or treacle. Molasses, the by-product of sugar-refining, had been available in England from the late thirteenth century when sugar was imported from Sicily. It was used by apothecaries for the making of theriaca, but was not generally available to the public. Then around 1650 the first big imports of sugar from the English colony of Barbados were brought to London refineries, which began to produce masses of cheap treacle, over and above that required by apothecaries and distillers. Now, poorer people, whose only affordable sweetener had been honey up until then, and that only on holidays, began to use 'common treacle' or 'London treacle', although they were slow to adopt it; significantly, one of their first uses for it was in the place of honey in the

21.
Coupons and labels:
(1) ingredients for
making parkin; (2)
Bonfire night fare;
(3) factory-baked
Scotch perkins.

FREE

SPEND £10 or more on GROCERIES
and get a 2lb tin of Syrup and a
500gm pack of Oatmeal FREE!

CONDITIONS OF USE: Only one voucher per
household, which must be presented at the check-out at
the time of purchase. Cannot be exchanged for cash. Not
redeemable for trade or bulk purchase. Altered or
defaced vouchers will not be accepted. Valid until
October 21, 1989. **LODGES SUPERMARKETS**

FREE

It's **BONFIRE TIME!**
GINGER BUNS 13p
GINGERBREAD MEN 17p
BONFIRE PARKIN 59p
FAMILY FAVOURITES from *Thurston*

SIMMERS
Bakers of
Traditional Biscuits
Scotch Ginger Perkins
SIMMERS, HATTON, ABERDEENSHIRE.
Baked in Scotland

making of gingerbread.[1] The re-instatement of fairs and festivals after the Restoration in 1660 would have seen an increase in gingerbread eating, especially as the price of ginger and other spices was reduced as a result of Britain finally getting its own spice routes.[2] Parkin is a kind of poor man's gingerbread, made with oatmeal instead of white wheat flour or white breadcrumbs, and made with or without spices. Just as with finer gingerbreads, the original parkin must have been made with honey. And just like them it probably had its origin in sacred food.

Because the mix of oatmeal, butter and honey is so very basic and obvious, the cake must have existed before it was given the name perkin/parkin, in any oat-growing area in Britain or elsewhere in northern Europe. Oats were introduced to the British Isles in the Iron Age, and both honey and butter could have been used at that time. These ingredients were always readily available – oats could be stored all year, honey also, and butter was kept for long periods buried in peat-bogs. Milk could have been included. The mixture could be eaten raw, or cooked on a hot hearthstone. This cake would not have been an everyday food, however, for until as late as 1700, it has been convincingly argued, sweetness was not a characteristic of everyday food.[3] A sweet tooth did not develop in Britain until the Middle Ages, and this only after the introduction of sugar in the late thirteenth century, imported in small quantities and bought and used sparingly only by the very rich; by Tudor times the wealthy class of Englishmen had become renowned across Europe for its sweet tooth. The common people did not eat sweet foods except at religious festivals and holiday times. Sugar was beyond their reach, and honey, though plentiful – up to the Reformation large quantities of beeswax were needed for monastery and church candles – was not cheap enough to be used more than occasionally. The average price per pound in the fifteenth century was 1¼d, but by the mid-sixteenth century two gallons cost 5/5d, and by 1580 the average price per pound was 3.4 pence.[4] Also, most of the honey especially in non-wine-growing areas, would be needed for fermentation into mead and similar drinks.

In northern Europe generally, honey was used in medicine and as a special food, but not as a general sweetener. There is plenty of evidence to suggest that up to the early eighteenth century in Germany, honey was eaten almost exclusively in fasting periods, and in Christmas baked foods;[5] and records give a similar picture for Britain. Its role was special to religious festivals. Honey was regarded anciently as sacred, literally a heavenly food, for it was produced by bees which were sacred creatures (considered chaste because they appeared to reproduce virginally).[6] The ceremonial combination of honey and milk is very ancient. They were offered to the dead in one of the oldest forms of ritual, and the offering of honey and milk as symbols of the heavenly and earthly was a usage at early Christian baptisms.[7] Honey cakes in the ancient world had very special significance and enjoyed sacred and sacrificial roles, and the German Lebkuchen, Pfefferkuchen and indeed all holiday gingerbreads and spicecakes may descend from these. The Lebkuchen was baked in early summer, and cooked till hard and dry, but kept until Christmas when it had become soft and chewy on account of the hygroscopic property of honey which enhances moisture retention and improves keeping qualities. So early honey cake 'came again', just as parkin is still said to do, and that must have given it the co-incidental extra virtue of rebirth or regeneration.[8] And so the evidence suggests that, perhaps until the early modern period, honey cake was a sacred or festival cake rather than an everyday one.

My interest in parkin was first aroused by the confusion caused by two names being used for it in the nineteenth century in parts of Lancashire and south Yorkshire: the other name is tharf cake. The unravelling of the significance of these two names has shed light on both, and

I hope it will go some way towards explaining why parkin is eaten on November 5th. The term tharf cake is of ancient Teutonic origin, although the cake itself is older than its name, being the most primitive kind of plain hearth cake. Anglo Saxon *theorf* or *tharf* means unfermented, unleavened, solid, tough, sodden. It was once the food of the poor countrywide, made of rough meal – oats, rye, barley – and water only, baked as flat cakes on the hearthstone or bakestone. It made hard eating. Piers Ploughman refers to the poor man's tharf cake. Wycliffe in his translation of the Gospels (1389) refers to tharf loaves frequently, meaning unleavened bread, e.g. Mark xiv v. 1 'Pask [Easter] and the feeste of therf looues was after the secunde day', and v. 12 'And the firste day of therue loues whenne pask was offrid'. It has been suggested that tharf cake was once eaten in association with Little Lent, on November 11th.[9] This was the autumnal fast of Martinmas which originally lasted for forty days until Christmas, and the rough, heavy nature of tharf cake would be appropriate to such a period of contrition and humility. But we have seen that honey could be added to fasting breads, both for its sacredness and as a special food to nourish those fasting;[10] its incorruptibility and its healing properties may also have been relevant. So holy-day tharf cake in northern Britain could have included honey and this would make it, therefore, materially the same as parkin.

The following November festivals illustrate the confusion of tharf cake/parkin. In some West Riding areas Parkin Sunday was the Sunday within the Octave of All Saints, so could occur on any of the first seven days in November, and in Lancashire Tharcake Monday was the last Monday after October 31st.[11] November 1st, All Hallows, was called Cake Night at Ripon, and Caking Day in Bradfield, Sheffield, when 'boys and young men dress themselves like mummers and go to farmhouses collecting money to buy tharf-cake with'. These tharf cakes in the nineteenth century were made with oatmeal, butter and treacle.[12] On

161

November 2nd, All Souls' Day, soul-mass-cakes were baked and given to the poor as an act of grace which was believed to alleviate the sufferings of the souls of the dead. In Lancashire soul-mass-cake was 'a kind of oatcakes', and in York it was a kind of parkin.[13] Tharf cake (perhaps sweetened with honey) could have been eaten at the old Martinmas Feast, November 11th, and, from the thirteenth century, the sweet and spiced variety would have been eaten at the Martilmas Fair also on November 11th (Old Style, November 23rd New Style). The Martilmas Fair was an important function, when cattle were bought and sold and servants hired for the coming year. It was also the time for killing the beasts to be salted for winter, and for feasting, dancing and merrymaking.

Since tharf cake/parkin was eaten on all these various dates, how did it come to be regarded as the special food of November 5th? The answer lies in the bonfire. The conglomeration of pagan and religious festivals in early November had long meant the baking of special cakes, and the lighting of bonfires, marking the beginning of winter. (Special cakes and bonfires were characteristic of all four of the Celtic Calendar festivals.) In some places, both tharf cake and the bonfire seem to have descended to us intact, in spite of later Christian intervention. Celtic festivals were Christianised as much as possible by the early church, for example, Samain, the Feast of the Dead on November 1st, was Christianised in A.D. 837 as All Hallows; but many Christian festivals retained elements of their pagan predecessors and indeed some pagan ceremonies were never wholly stamped out, especially in remote or wild regions. The grim Samain bonfires of November 1st survived in several areas, and when Guy Fawkes in 1605 gave the English a legitimate excuse for a bonfire it was joyfully seized upon as if there were some deep need, and held in most places on November 5th; but in other places the old survivals remained on November 1st. It seems natural that the holy-day/holiday cake that had long been associated with various festivals in early November – the sacred Celtic breads which had been adopted by the Christians – should also be eaten at this bonfire. However, I have not found any evidence to suggest that parkin was eaten specifically on November 5th before the nineteenth century. This may be because up to the nineteenth century November 5th had been but one holiday among many, but by the time of industrialisation, had become one of the few remaining holidays – for many seasonal and religious holidays associated with what had once been a largely agricultural way of life had died out. It now seems incredible, but up to 1838, many workers were granted only the afternoons of Good Friday and Christmas Day as holidays.[14] Therefore Guy Fawkes' Night assumed greater importance. Hone wrote that to poor boys, 'on account of its festivous enjoyment [it] is the greatest holiday of the season'.[15] As a holiday it required its special food, and so in many northern areas parkin filled that role, along with treacle toffee (Tom Trot) and potatoes roasted in the bonfire. In Leeds the cake, rather than Guy Fawkes, gave its name to November 5th, which was there called Parkin Day.[16]

But the people had long forgotten what they were really celebrating. Even when tharf cake/parkin was eaten in the nineteenth century, supposedly in celebration of November 5th, it was, in parts of the West Riding, eaten also a few days afterwards (for a forgotten Martinmas?);[17] and in other places eaten in the few days before, perhaps in an unbroken tradition from the Iron Age, via All Hallows and All Souls, as the following might indicate:

> On the 5th of November parkin, a sort of pepper-cake, made with treacle and ginger, is found in every house in the West Riding. As, however, the cake is eaten several days before the 5th, I have no doubt it originally formed part of the All-Hallows' feast.[18]

The All Hallows cake is the pagan Samain bannock, Christianised. Many British Celtic rituals survived long and are well-recorded. In Scotland, the old Highland Quarter Cakes (accompanied by bonfires) were '*the bonnach Bride*, St Bride's bannock, baked for the first day of spring [February 1st]; the *bonnach Bealtain*, Beltane bannock, baked for the first day of summer [May 1st]; the *bonnach Lunastain*, Lammas bannock, baked for the first day of autumn [August 1st]; and the *bonnach Samhthaim*, Hallowmas bannock, baked for the first day of winter [November 1st]'.[19] At each of these four major Calendar festivals (of which Samain was the most important) the 'flat round cake or bannock was the focal point of the feast, and its allocation to the man or woman, or couple, who would have the honour of breaking it and distributing it amongst the people was attended by much ritual and clear sexual undertones . . . it was usually a communal performance'.[20] John Ray in his 1674 glossary *North Country Words* defines bannock as 'an oatcake kneaded with water only, and baked in embers'. If made with barley it was a 'bere-bannock'. The ritual bannock was usually enriched with extra ingredients. At the Christianised pagan festival on the eve of St Michael (September 29th) a cake called *struan Micheil* was still being made in the West of Scotland at the end of the nineteenth century – it was made of the newly harvested oats, rye or barley (whatever corn was grown on the croft), ground and mixed with milk, berries and wild honey. One was made for each absent or dead family member. It was shared ritually among the family.[21] In Ross-shire in the late nineteenth century, the *struan Micheil* was made with the new corn, and enriched with eggs, butter and treacle (it was therefore virtually parkin). The dough was cooked on the hot hearthstone under an inverted pot. After keeping some for the household, the housewife shared the rest among the neighbours, 'there being great rivalry as to who should be the first to grind the new meal and get the struan ready. The first to do so was generally understood to have the best crops through the coming year'.[22] A parkin-like cake is recorded in Orkney in the late nineteenth century. The folklorist Marian McNeill describes, in 1929, the cake she ate in her childhood called 'Broonie', made with oatmeal, flour, butter, treacle, sugar etc., and the recipe as she reconstructs it 'Orkney Oatmeal Gingerbread' is indistinguishable from English parkin, except that it is mixed with buttermilk.[23] The Scottish National Dictionary defines Brunie as a scone or bannock of barley or oatmeal, made in Orkney, 'a thick cake which may be rendered "short" by the use of fat (1888)'. The word is from Norwegian bryne – a slice of bread or cake, a mutated form of brunn, brown – from the colour of a baked bannock, cognisant with English burn. 'Small cakes very round and thick, named Broonies' are also recorded in Shetland 1822.[24]

In Yorkshire, pagan ritual is more eroded and not always so easily recognisable, though in north Yorkshire, where parkin was 'a flat cake of gingerbread', the November 5th bonfire was clearly embrangled with ancient superstition. There the lads sang various doggerel verses while dragging their wood and branches to the bonfire site. This one from Great Ayton in the eighteenth century has much more to do with a pagan god or demon than with Guy Fawkes:

> Au'd Grimey sits upon yon hill
> Ez black ez onny au'd craw;
> He's gitten on his lang grey coat
> Wi' buttons doon afoor-oor-oor, [3 times]
> He's gitten on his lang grey coat
> Wi' buttons doon afoor.[25]

In the Pennine hills near Sheffield, echoes of an ancient rite remained till the nineteenth century. Here, tharf cake was eaten in November but not necessarily on the 5th. In the following account, the reason for the ritual has long been forgotten:

It was usual to save money for making tharf-cakes. People would subscribe so much each, say a halfpenny a week, towards a fund for making these cakes. The cakes were eaten in November, first at one man's house, and the next year at another man's house. Thus the neighbours in their turn held a little yearly feast. These entertainments were called 'tharf-cake joinings'. At the thar-cake, or tharf-cake joinings in Hathersage it was customary to keep a bit of the cake from one November to the next.[26]

At Bradwell, four miles from Hathersage, on November 5th, they divided the tharf cake among the family – father, mother, brothers and sisters – calling this a thar-cake joining. People would say 'Have you joined yet?' meaning 'Have you made your thar-cake yet?'. Children at Bradwell would club together to buy meal and treacle, and ask somebody to make the cake for them.[27] At Bradfield, near Sheffield, as we have seen, on November 1st youths dressed as mummers went round farmhouses collecting money to buy tharf cake with. And on November 5th again in the Sheffield area, where tharf cake was 'a circular cake':

At the bonfires, the young folks club pence, and then buy oatmeal and treacle, which the lads pay for, and the girls make into cakes. When baked, and sometimes only half-done, being cross-marked in the dough, they are broken into halves and quarters, and still further sub-divided if large, being broken by hand betwixt the lad and lass – always in halves.[28]

This remnant of ritual recalls the allocating of sacred bread at Celtic festivals which had 'clear sexual undertones'. In the same area in the eighteenth century Samuel Pegge wrote: 'Thar-cake, 'Tis made of the *first* oatmeal, with water and sugar or treacle' [my italics] although it is just possible that 'first' referred to the quality of the oatmeal rather than the first meal from the recently harvested crop.[29] In other parts of Yorkshire the parkin party took place among schoolchildren. On November 5th in Nidderdale schools (Lofthouse and Middlesmoor) the master was barred out by the scholars until he granted a half-day holiday; a collection was then taken among the scholars for parkin ingredients, and a parkin party followed, an equal number of small parkins being allotted to each child. In Huddersfield the headmaster of Almondbury Grammar School was given presents of parkin by parents and others. At Midhope near Sheffield the schoolmaster received so many parkins he was still eating them behind his desk lid the following May.[30]

Why should the ancient term tharf cake for this sweetened oatcake remain in parts of Lancashire, north Derbyshire and south Yorkshire, and yet the later term perkin or parkin be adopted in the regions to the north of this area? There is no explanation for the adoption of the newer term, but it seems possible that it comes from Perkin or Parkin, the man's Christian name (a diminutive of the Old French Piers), which was popular between 1250 and 1500–1550, after which the modern form Peter took its place.[31] Perkin was a common name, and so as applied to a cake it could imply the cake was common also, much like the later Brown George, Brown Tommy, Flat Dick or Johnny Cake, which are all rough breads. These names display affectionate disdain for the breads people were forced to eat when there was nothing better. They would much rather have been eating white bread. Similarly parkin-eaters would much rather have been eating the finest gingerbread, full of candied peel, coriander seeds, caraways, cloves, cinnamon, ginger, mace and nutmeg, moulded in fancy shapes and covered in gold leaf.[32] This adoption of the 'vulgar' name Perkin for a formerly sacred cake could have occurred in the early thirteenth century at the time when holy days had become holidays, when for instance, the solemn fast of St Martin on November 11th had given way to the secular feasting of the Martilmas Fair, and when the reverent wake was becoming the rowdy wakes.[33]

At this time spices would have been affordable by the less well-off, bought at holiday time only, the cheaper among them being ginger, cinnamon and pepper; ginger and pepper had been available before the Conquest, probably being first imported by the Romans.[34] Honey was being produced in quantity – the church was still expanding, and prospering commercially, and it needed its candles.

From the early seventh century, eastern Lowland Scotland as far north as the Firth of Forth, had been part of the kingdom of Northumbria, and there people spoke not Gaelic, but a dialect of English. There perkin was, and is, the name for the sweet oatmeal cake, which even today takes the form of individual small flat cakes – biscuits (with an almond on top) which indicates long use of hearth, bakestone or griddle rather than oven.[35] These perkins spread to other parts of Scotland. Similar perkins are also still made in Northumberland. In modern Durham and Yorkshire, Cumberland, Westmorland, Lancashire, and Cheshire the term parkin is used, and shows the same vowel shift -er to -ar as in clerk, Berkshire, Derby etc.[36] The hearth, bakestone or griddle would also have been used here, and the biscuit variety is still occasionally made, but in these areas today parkin is usually a large slab-like cake, baked in an oven. North Derbyshire Thor cakes (pronounced thar) still remain in the older small flat round form only as hard biscuits.[37]

The terms tharf cake/parkin were used interchangeably in Lancashire and south Yorkshire for about fifty years until the 1890s, when the older term tharf cake fell out of use and the newly adopted term parkin remained; tharf cake was too grim a reminder to the mass of the population of their long subsistence on oatmeal, including hard, plain tharf cake. Times were especially hard from the 1790s to the 1840s. Addy, in 1888, was amazed that a shopkeeper in a good street in Sheffield only a few years previously had still been advertising tharf cake for sale in his window, for, says Addy, 'I find that people are ashamed of tharf-cake. They call it parkin instead of using the old word.'[38]

In 1674 Ray had defined tharf cakes as 'the same with Bannocks, viz. Cakes made of Oat-meal and fair Water, without Yeast or Leaven, and so baked.' Their inclusion in Ray's glossary indicates that they survived only in the north at this date. Tharf cake in this original simple form continued widely in the north side by side with sweet tharf cake/parkin until the 1840s, when the plain sort was thankfully abandoned. The English Dialect Dictionary describes plain tharf cake of the early nineteenth century as 'an unleavened cake of flour or meal, mixed with milk or water, rolled out thin and baked' (from Derbyshire northwards); 'Baked on the hearth among the embers' (Durham and Cumberland), giving as illustration: (Northumberland) 'They never gat owse better than thaaf keahyk'; 'A thicker tharf-cake was sometimes made of hinder-end wheat, pea-meal, and dressed "chisel".' In Almondbury, Huddersfield, tharf cake was called waterparkin or waterfirling.[39] In the Lancashire village of Bradshaw, near Bolton, plain tharf cake was still eaten about 1840. A correspondent to the Manchester City News wrote:

> Tharcake with us consisted of oatmeal and water, sometimes with a little dripping, and sometimes without, and it was baked over the fire on an oven plate or on a backstone. Parkin was unknown. When treacle was added we called it treacle cake, or treacle bunnock. Tharcake was made at various times all the year round when other bread ran short; treacle cake or treacle bunnock just before the fifth of November, and very seldom at any other time.

In the area between Manchester and Oldham in the same period it was called th'ard cake, a term which made sense to its eaters on account of its hardness. The softer cake called parkin seems to have been introduced there by commercial bakers who from the 1840s flourished in every town to supply baked goods for women mill-workers who had no time to bake (in contrast, in Yorkshire, women mill-workers were expected to stay at home after marriage, and to bake all their own bread and cakes):

> Th'ard cake, meaning, as I always understood, 'the hard cake' . . . as made at home in all the townships between Manchester and Oldham, was hard enough thirty or forty years ago. The shop, or soft variety, made by professional confectioners, more often received the name of parkin about the same time. Hence, perhaps, the more common use now of the term Parkin, since even the common people make it [1885]. Parkin is invariably baked in tins. Th'ardcake was often baked in cakes on the oven bottom.[40]

These examples do seem to indicate that the term parkin for the sweet cake occurred originally north of a line going east to west from the Humber.

The first mention I have found of parkin is in a ballad, probably composed in the seventeenth century, about a merry wedding in the time of Robin Hood; it is the 'Song of Arthur o' Bradley':

> When Arthur, to make their hearts merry
> Brought ale and parkin and perry . . .[41]

Although it refers to the fourteenth century, it cannot be taken as proof that the word parkin existed at that time. The first definitely dated reference to parkin I have collected is 1728. The working people had developed a sweet tooth by about 1700, aided by supplies of cheap treacle, which in the greater part of the north must have been a welcome addition to a very monotonous though fairly healthy diet, consisting largely of oatmeal. Parkin was being made in the Halifax area in 1728, as this piece of information given at the West Riding Quarter Sessions by one Anne Whittaker shows. In haytime of that year:

> her Mistress did persuade her to ask Sarah Preistley Mr Nicholl's Town Apprentice to steale Meal from her Master to make a parkin on . . . sent the meal by a Little Lad . . . her Mistress also gave the sd Sarah Preistley some brass to ffetch Treakle with from Elland to make a parkin with . . . but her Mistress Ann Man made Pottage with the Meal.

It seems the judge did not know what parkin was because the document has the explanation 'parkins alias cakes'. He may not have been a northerner. However, even a northern judge may not have been conversant with the foodways of the labouring and tradesmen classes.[42]

In the 1740s the Lancashire weaver Tim Bobbin describes 'therf cake' as being made of oatmeal, unleavened, mixed with butter and treacle, the Lancashire expression of that date 'As thodd'n as o Thar-Cake' describes its density and heaviness.[43] These foregoing examples indicate that everyday parkin did not include ginger or other spice; that would have been a holiday addition. It is clear from the Halifax case that parkin was made all year round, and not in November only. A further illustration occurs in 1802 at the Moravian Settlement at Fulneck, Pudsey, near Leeds; the elders had been exercised about a local woman selling her baked goods on a Sunday to Pudsey children who came to the Moravian Sunday School:

> Many of the Girls and boys who frequent the Single Sisters buy tarts and parkin of her on Sundays, and it would seem hard if they were not allowed them as some bring little else for their Dinners. It was proposed that Susannah Brooke be permitted to sell only on Sunday her cakes and pastry.[44]

171

Note that parkin is in the singular, which is sometimes used as a collective term for a number of small parkins, but I think here implies a large cake which could have been baked in the oven after the tarts (they require different heats). In Todmorden in the period up to 1840, parkin often constituted the entire dinner of poor people, as a change from porridge or potatoes. This dinner was:

> a share of *parkin*, none too big, baked on the
> backstone and chover [chafing dish of hot coals],
> with a pot of pennyroyal . . . or mint *teah*, sweetened
> with treacle. That was a good dinner if the *parkin*
> had suet in it, and needed no dessert to follow.[45]

It was even served at funerals. At a late nineteenth-century funeral on the North York Moors, the 'quality' were served with good old port and sponge cake, and the 'many' with mulled ale and parkin.[46]

Considering the rarity of ovens, and that many places did not even have a public baker or public oven until the 1820s, thar cake/parkin must have been made widely on a bakestone or griddle, or in a frying pan, well into the nineteenth century (or on an oven sheet placed over the fire, as at Bolton in Lancashire). Alternatively, it could have been cooked in cakes large or small, thick or thin, under an upturned cauldron or yetling on the hearth, surrounded by burning peats. Parkin requires careful cooking, or the treacle (or honey) burns. It is impossible to reproduce the exact taste and texture of that earlier parkin today as modern oatmeal, because of the heat treatment used to stabilise it, has less moisture content; and old molasses, because of cruder refining techniques, was sweeter than ours, and so pound for pound, less pungent.[47] Nevertheless, by adding a drop of milk and using half black treacle, half dark syrup, it is possible to approximate taste and texture, and to produce hard biscuits, thin scones, or a large cake one inch or more thick, all done on an iron griddle or in an iron pan, or in the oven. The method of making parkin around 1830 (which could have been the same for a hundred and fifty years, or much longer if one substitutes honey for treacle) is described in 1884 by Miss E. Ferrand of Brockholes near Huddersfield. The season's new meal was used, if possible, which was at its best at the end of October (and it tasted its best straight from the drying kiln); the preference for new meal was probably here one of taste rather than ritual:

> Meal, of course, is the principal ingredient in parkin, and my mother always made a point of having the new meal made and brought home from the corn mill in time to make the parkin. And it was parkin and no mistake, in those days. Lard and milk were *non est* [unobtainable], butter nearly so, but there was plenty of ginger, eight pounds of treacle for a family of eight, and as much meal as could be stirred in, or driven in. I am speaking of the time when I used to watch my mother make that quantity, when I was a little girl, after having grated her the ginger; and it was extremely hard work working the quantity of meal into that mass. This kind of parkin was dense, close, and compact, but also very good.[48]

Ginger was still the cheapest spice: in 1800 when nutmegs cost £5 16s 0d. per lb, dried root ginger was only 1s 8d. per lb.[49] Suet, dripping or lard was used when butter was unavailable. Baking soda had been used in America from about 1800, but it was not until the later 1840s that baking soda and baking powders were used in Yorkshire with any regularity, when the almost simultaneous advent of cheap flour and sugar along with cast iron ovens and plenty of cheap fuel started the northern baking bonanza.[50] Flour began to be added to parkin, and this lightened the heavy cake. After 1880, Lyle's Golden Syrup altered the taste even further. The heavy type of parkin, when not eaten fresh, had to be kept for at least two weeks on a shelf to soften (not in a tin, which dried it). So for weeks before November 5th the wonderful smell of baking parkins drifted out of doorways. They were made 'as big as a pavin' stooan' and 'as big as th'oven could hold.'[51] There were three types in West Yorkshire: 'Meyl parkin contains a greater quantity of oatmeal than does "treacle parkin", and "flahr parkin" has a good deal of flour in it in addition to treacle'.[52] Thick flour parkin was called 'moggy' which stuck to the roof of the mouth; but in the West Riding flour parkin was never as popular as meal or treacle parkin. An advantage of meal or treacle parkin was that it could be eaten raw or half-cooked by the impatient, as the example of the Sheffield young folks proves. In fact old-fashioned heavy parkin should be slightly underdone in the middle so that it stays fudgy or sad. Parkin is generally preferred moist or 'weyky' and sticky, never dry. There is no joy in eating dry parkin.

The eating of parkin in massive quantities was declining by the end of the nineteenth century. The rising standard of living and the great variety of alternative confectionery reduced the demand for gingerbreads of all kinds. In 1877 the Yorkshire Clock Almanack compared modern parkin eating with that in the 1840s: 'Ther isn't as mitch traitl parkin etten bi monny a booat looad as ther wor then'.[53] Because parkin remained for so long a very simple mixture of ingredients, I have not found any recipes before the nineteenth century; but there are plenty from the mid-nineteenth century when flour and baking powders were introduced. In M. Gaskell's *A Yorkshire Cookery Book* produced in Wakefield in 1919 there are no fewer than seventeen for parkin. There are still many different kinds of parkin made in homes in the north, every family having its own recipe, some favouring a preponderance of flour to oats, some a preponderance of treacle. Some parkins are still made without raising agent, and some are mixed with beer or spirits instead of milk, and often need long keeping in order to become palatable. But the genus parkin remains popular, regarded as pleasing, filling and cheap; and parkin in the form of slabs, squares, buns, biscuits and parkin pigs, according to the district, are still displayed in bakers' windows, and are still enjoyed most especially around November 5th.[54]

The first four recipes are conjectural reconstructions which I have tried out.

Recipes

Plain tharf cake or bannock

To 2 heaped tablespoons of medium oatmeal add enough cold water or milk to make a thick dough. Roll out on scattered meal into one round, or several, ¼" or less thick. Cook in a pre-heated, ungreased heavy iron frying pan, or on an iron griddle, extremely gently, for about 30 minutes or until dried out. Use a pansaver or trivet if necessary. Cool on a cake rack.

These cakes remain hard even if left out on a shelf for months.

Hard honey tharf cakes/parkins

These are plain tharf cakes, slightly sweetened, of the type which were probably made at holiday times by the poor.

8 oz oatmeal
²/₃ cup milk
1 large tablespoon honey
ginger or black pepper (optional)

Gently melt the honey, if thick, in the milk. Add meal to make a very stiff dough. Press into several 3" diameter cakes, about ¼" thick. Heat an ungreased heavy iron frying pan or griddle, and sprinkle a little meal over the hot surface, then place the cakes carefully on this, and cook extremely gently for an hour or more till dried out and hard, but not browned too much. If damp patches are left the cakes will not keep. These remain hard and brittle even when stored for several months on an open shelf. (The spices named were available only after the Roman Conquest, but may not have been affordable by the poorer people until the Middle Ages.)

A Bakestone parkin with honey

I have reconstructed this cake on the lines of the 1830 treacle parkin as described by Miss Ferrand; it was perhaps made like this up to the end of the seventeenth century.

8 oz honey
2 oz butter
12 oz medium oatmeal
1 tbs milk (optional)
butter for greasing
ginger, allspice, black pepper (optional)

Gently melt the butter and honey and mix in the other ingredients. Well butter an iron frying pan or griddle and press the stiff mixture in to form one cake ¾" thick. Be sure to place the pan or griddle over a pansaver, and cook one hour as gently as possible. Do not allow the honey to burn. Then cut into quarters or smaller pieces and turn each piece to cook the other side, each time adding more butter to the pan. Cook 10 or 15 minutes more. It is done when no wet bits are apparent. Tender, if eaten fresh, it hardens somewhat on cooling, but softens if left on a shelf for several weeks.

This honey cake is too tender to turn over all in one piece, and so originally it may have been cooked on a hot hearthstone covered with an inverted pot with hot peats piled around it, or even simply left on the bakestone or hearth for much longer, to dry out completely. Alternatively, the top could have been finished off with a hot shovel or salamander.

A Bakestone parkin with treacle

I have based this reconstructed recipe on the description given for parkin as made about 1830 by Miss Ferrand of Brockholes, Huddersfield.

> 5 oz black treacle
> 5 oz Dark Syrup
> 4 oz fat (½ butter, ½ lard)
> 1¼–1½ lbs medium oatmeal
> 3 tsp ground ginger or grated dry ginger root
> 2 tbs milk
> a little lard for greasing

Gently melt the fat and treacles, and mix with the other ingredients to make a very thick dough which will stay in shape when a spoonful is put on a plate. (Leaving it overnight thickens it.) Add more meal if too thin. Melt a little lard gently in a 9" diameter heavy iron frying pan, spoon the mixture in and flatten to make one large cake about 1" thick. A heavy pan is essential and very gentle heat and watching is necessary, as the treacle will burn if too hot, and then the parkin will be spoilt. If you can smell the treacle, turn the heat down, or place the pan on a pansaver or trivet. After 30 minutes turn the cake over by clapping the back of a larded oven sheet over the pan and inverting, re-lard the frying pan, and slip the inverted cake back in, to do very slowly for another 15 minutes or more. If using an iron girdle, do as the Sheffield youngsters did, and mark your raw cake, once it is on the girdle, with a cross, so it is easy to break it in halves and quarters when you want to invert it. The dough can be eaten at this or any stage, even raw, because there is no flour in it. The finished cake will have a slightly crunchy top and bottom and a soft middle. Small parkins may be made by flattening spoonfuls of mixture in the hot larded pan or on the greased griddle to about a centimetre thick (they may be as thin or thick as you please). Alternatively, the mixture may be pressed into a 1½" thick cake on a well-larded baking sheet and baked at gas mark 4, 350°F (180°C) for about 40 minutes (it will spread a little). It should not be allowed to get too brown at the edges; turn the heat down if necessary. It tastes best eaten while still warm, or after two weeks on a shelf, when it will be found to have softened or 'come again'.

Treacle parkin, oven-baked

This recipe dates from the mid-nineteenth century. It tastes like treacle toffee.

1 lb treacle (½ black treacle, ½ Dark Syrup)
8 oz butter
1½ lbs medium oatmeal
8 oz brown sugar
1 tsp ginger
1 tsp allspice

Gently warm the butter and treacle until only just melted, then mix with the dry ingredients. Well grease a tin measuring about 7½x9½x2" and bake at gas mark 2, 300°F (150°C) for 2 hours. It is done if it springs back when touched, although it is nicest if still very slightly underdone in the centre.

Beer parkin, Yorkshire

Mid-nineteenth century: the addition of flour, egg, beer and baking soda transforms it into a soft cake.

Prodigal Frugality

8 oz plain flour
1 tsp bicarbonate of soda
2 tsp ginger
8 oz medium oatmeal
6 oz fat (mixed butter and lard)
1 lb black treacle
½ pint strong beer (e.g. Guinness or Theakston's
Old Peculier)
1 egg, beaten

Mix treacle and beer and warm very gently. Sift flour, soda and ginger, add the oatmeal and rub the fat in, add the beer, treacle and egg and mix well. Well grease a tin measuring about 7½x9½x2". Bake at gas mark 4, 350°F (180°C) for an hour. Eat this one within two weeks.

I make mine in an enamelled tin so that the cake need not be removed for storage.

A Modern Parkin

This recipe is from my family in Huddersfield. Dark Syrup, sometimes called Amber Syrup, helps give it its specially nice flavour. If unobtainable, use half black treacle, half golden syrup.

8 oz butter
8 oz Dark Syrup
8 oz self-raising flour
4 tsp ginger
8 oz medium oatmeal
8 oz demerara sugar
2 eggs
¼ pint milk

Gently warm the butter and syrup, till only just melted. Beat the eggs and mix with the milk. In a large bowl sift the flour and ginger, mix with the sugar and oatmeal, then add the butter and syrup, the

179

eggs and milk, and mix well to a sloppy batter. Well grease a tin measuring about 7½x9½x2", and pour in the batter. Bake in the middle of the oven at gas mark 3, 325°F (170°C) for one hour only. The edges will be slightly crisp, and the centre tender. Modern parkin should be kept in an airtight tin.

I cook mine in an enamel tin so the cake can stay in it for storage.

Thor cakes, Derbyshire

For November 5th, from Wirksworth near Bakewell. Recipe re-worded from *Derbyshire Cookery, recipes collected by Janet Arthur* (Dalesman Books 1976), p. 42. This is another modern recipe.

1 lb fine oatmeal
1 lb plain flour
1 lb sugar
2 tsp baking powder
1 tsp coriander seeds
1 tsp salt (I leave this out)
1 tsp ginger
2 oz candied peel
12 oz butter
1 lb warmed treacle

Sift flour, baking powder and ginger, and mix with the other dry ingredients except the candied peel. Rub in the butter, add the treacle and peel. Knead a little, roll out fairly thin, and cut into large rounds about 4" in diameter. Bake in a moderate oven gas mark 4, 350°F (180°C) till golden.

The flavour of lard in the following three kinds of biscuits is somewhat crude for modern tastes.

Prodigal Frugality

Thor cakes, Derbyshire

For November 5th; Mrs Nixon, White Lodge Cottage,
Baslow near Bakewell; recipe collected about 1940 by
Dr Bedford (Bedford MSS 432/4 p. 56, Leeds
University Brotherton Library.) This quantity makes
a large amount:

> 2 lbs fine oatmeal
> 3 tbs sugar
> 8 oz lard
> 1 tsp baking powder
> 1 tsp ginger

Make into paste with treacle. Stamp in rounds, bake
in moderate oven.
(Rub lard in, use about 3 tbs treacle, roll the biscuit
dough to ¼" thick, cut into rounds and bake at gas
mark 4, 350°F (180°C) for 25–30 minutes. Leave a
minute before removing to a cooling tray.)

Yorkshire Parkins

Mrs A. Eley, Snydale, Wakefield, from M. M. Gaskell,
A Yorkshire Cookery Book 4th edn. (Wakefield 1919)
p. 95 (re-worded):

> 4 oz plain flour
> 2 tsp ginger
> 2 tsp mixed spice
> 8 oz oatmeal
> 4 oz brown sugar
> 4 oz lard
> 4 oz treacle (dark)
> ½ tsp bicarbonate of soda
> 1 tbs milk

Sift flour and spices, mix with oatmeal and sugar and
rub in the lard. Add the treacle. Mix the soda in the
milk, add, and mix the whole very well to a light

paste. Scatter some meal, and form the mixture into rounds ½" thick and place well apart on larded baking trays. Bake at gas mark 2, 300°F (150°C) for about 25 minutes. Loosen the biscuits but leave a minute before transferring to a cooling tray.

Scotch Perkins

Re-worded from *Aunt Kate's Day-By-Day Book* (London and Dundee, 1936) p. 71:

4 oz plain flour
½ tsp bicarbonate of soda
½ tsp salt
½ tsp cinnamon
½ tsp ginger
¼ tsp mixed spice
4 oz fine oatmeal
3 oz sugar
2 oz lard
3 oz syrup and treacle mixed
a few almonds, blanched

Sift the flour, soda, salt and spices, mix with the oatmeal and sugar. Warm the treacle and lard gently till only just melted. Make a stiff dough, form into walnut-sized balls, place well apart on greased trays and press half a blanched almond in the centre of each. Bake at gas mark 3, 325°F (170°C) for 15–20 minutes. Makes about 20. (I prefer to omit the salt.)

Notes and References

County names and divisions referred to throughout are those in existence before the boundary changes of 1974.

1. Sydney W. Mintz, *Sweetness and Power* (London, 1985), p. 37; C. Anne Wilson, *Food and Drink in Britain* (Penguin, 1976), pp. 273–4; E. Smith, *The Compleat Housewife* (London, 1727), p. 130.
2. Wilson, p. 262. In 1696–7 ginger constituted 67% of total spices imported into Britain, mostly from the West Indies. Its wholesale

price was only 1¾d per lb. (Colin S. Dence, 'Long Pepper (II)', *Petits Propos Culinaires* 7, p. 65.)

3. Eva Crane, *Honey* (London, 1975), p. 474. The teeth in the seven hundred victims of the bubonic plague of 1349, whose skeletons were found near the Tower of London in 1987, show few signs of decay.

4. Crane, pp. 471; 473.

5. M. D. Bindley, 1965, 'Some contemporary records of early honey production and use', *Bee World* 46 (1), pp. 32–3: account books from hospitals in Mainz, Munich and Augsburg between 1493 and 1732, quoted by Crane, p. 472.

6. Crane, p. 469.

7. Crane, p. 386.

8. There is a saying, still current, that people who find a new lease of life have 'come again, like parkin.'

9. S. O. Addy, *A Glossary of Words used in the Neighbourhood of Sheffield* (English Dialect Society, 1888), p. 254.

10. In an experiment it was found that a man could live for three months without too much deprivation on nothing but milk and honey, Crane, p. 263.

11. Leeds Mercury Weekly Supplement, Local Notes and Queries, 19 February 1881; J. H. Nodal and G. Milner, *A Glossary of the Lancashire Dialect* (English Dialect Society, 1875–82).

12. Addy p. 254; Rev. Joseph Hunter, *The Hallamshire Glossary* (London, 1829).

13. W. Hone wrote that on November 2nd the wealthy in Lancashire dispense oaten cake called soul-mass-cake to the poor, *Table Book* (London, c.1850), p. 347; George Benson, *Customs of York* (Burdekin printer, York) (no page numbers).

14. Leeds Mercury Weekly Supplement, Local Notes and Queries, 22 December 1888.

15. W. Hone, *The Everyday Book*, 2 vols. (London, 1826), I, p. 719.

16. A. R. Wright, ed. T. E. Lones, *British Calendar Customs, England*, Vol III (Folk-Lore Society, London and Glasgow, 1940), p. 151; C. C. Robinson, *The Dialect of Leeds* (London, 1862).

17. A. Easther, *A Glossary of the Dialect of Almondbury and Huddersfield* (English Dialect Society, 1883). The Huddersfield diarist John Turner wrote on November 6th 1750 'Gave wife for treacle for a parkin, 1d'. Diary of John Turner, Huddersfield Local History Library. On November 6th, 1800, Dorothy Wordsworth in Grasmere, Cumberland, wrote 'I was baking bread, dinner, and parkins.' *Journals of Dorothy Wordsworth*, ed. Helen Darbishire (London, 1958), p. 66.

18. Note by S. Baring-Gould in William Henderson, *Folklore of the Northern Counties* (Folk-Lore Society, London, 1879), p. 97.

19. F. M. McNeill, *The Scots Kitchen* (London and Glasgow, reprinted 1968), p. 185.

20. I. M. Stead, J. B. Bourke, Don Brothwell, *Lindow Man the Body in the Bog* (British Museum Publications, 1986), pp. 164–5.

21. ibid., p. 165.

22. Sheila MacDonald, 'Old World Survivals in Ross-shire', *Folk-Lore*, 1903, pp. 381–2.
23. McNeill, pp. 206–7.
24. Supplement to Scottish National Dictionary.
25. R. Blakeborough, *Yorkshire Wit, Character, Folklore and Customs of The North Riding of Yorkshire* (London, 1898), pp. 86–7.
26. S. O. Addy, *Household Tales and Traditional Remains* (London and Sheffield, 1895), p. 129.
27. Wright and Lones, p. 152.
28. Addy, *Glossary*; Yorkshire Weekly Post, 29 March 1884, p. 3 col. 3.
29. Samuel Pegge, *Two Collections of Derbicisms* (English Dialect Society, 1896), p. 73.
30. Peter Brears, *Traditional Food in Yorkshire* (Edinburgh, 1987), p. 171; Easther, p. 97.
31. Personal communication from Dr George Redmonds.
32. Some parkin recipes contain coriander or caraway seeds, candied peel or allspice etc., usually no more than one of these additions.
33. Fairs or 'tides' were established on Saints' days e.g. in the West Riding, Emley Fair was officially established in 1254, Almondbury Martinmas Fair in 1294. The Wake was originally a prayerful watch kept all night before the day of the Saint to whom the parish church was dedicated. This also degenerated into merrymaking – the wake or feast – about this time. The OED gives 1225 as its earliest example.
34. Wilson p. 254; Elizabeth David, *Spices, Salt and Aromatics in the English Kitchen* (Penguin, 1977), p. 33.
35. In Scotland November 5th is not such a popular celebration as it is in England, and perkins are not particularly attached to it. Hallowe'en remains the important November festival in Scotland.
36. All over England and Lowland Scotland the Christian name was Perkin till about 1400, when it started to change to Parkin, and by the 1500s (in the West Riding and most probably elsewhere in England) had completely changed to Parkin (Personal communication from Dr George Redmonds).
37. Bedford MSS 432/4 p. 56, Brotherton Library, University of Leeds. Thor is a misnomer. 'Treacle cakes, or "parkins" . . . are universally called "t'harff cake" at and about Sheffield.' (Yorkshire Weekly Post, March 29 1884, p. 3.) The spelling shows how those with some education tried to rationalise the dialect words they heard, e.g. 'th' could be rationalised as the definite article, so that th'ar cake might be thought to be Har cake. Sheila Hutchins in *Grannie's Kitchen*, Mayflower, 1979, p. 152 says 'Lancashire parkin used to be called Harcake or Soul Mass Cake . . . Har is the Norse name for the pagan god Odin. It all goes back to the pagan winter festival'. Also in Derbyshire: 'local authorities suggest that this date, [November 5th], co-incides with an old feast held in honour of the Scandinavian god

Thor.' (Wright and Lones, p. 152.) The fact that Derbyshire people spell their cakes Thor (always with a capital T), but Derbyshire country people pronounced it thar, puts the name under the same suspicion of having been rationalised comparatively recently; and the fact that the English Dialect Dictionary lists neither Har nor Thor would seem to support this. Also Thor is not phonetically acceptable for this area (personal communication from Stanley Ellis). Th'ard cake, supposedly meaning 'the hard cake' was in use in both Lancashire and West Yorkshire.

38. Addy, *Glossary*, p. 254. The expression 'as tough as bull-liver and thar-cake' survived to the mid-twentieth century in the Peak District, cf. Brian Woodall, *Calendar of Events, Peak District* (Sheffield, 1976).

39. Easther, *Glossary*.

40. Both examples are from Manchester City News, *Notes and Queries*, Vol. 6, 1885–6, p. 11. Soft, cakey parkin spread to Westmorland and the Lake Counties via Lancashire and the Craven district of Yorkshire.

41. An earlier black letter version, which mentions different comestibles, and does not include parkin, is printed by Joseph Ritson, *Robin Hood*, 1795, II p. 210. The dating of ballads can be problematical. The later version, which mentions parkin, is quoted in W. Carr *The Dialect of Craven* (London, 1828), p. 45.

42. The following February the dismissed Sarah Preistley aged 12 or 13 was persuaded by one Mary Clay to help break into Nicholl's house on several successive nights to steal food; 'they both went in at the casement, Made Parkins of meal which the[y] found in a Bowl.' 'They eat all but some parkin wch Sarah Preistley took with her into a hay mow.' 1729 was a dear year when the poor starved. W.R.Q.S. 1/68/4 Informations, West Yorkshire Archive Service, Wakefield. This source kindly given by Dr George Redmonds.

43. John Collier, *The Miscellaneous Works of Tim Bobbin Esq., containing his View of the Lancashire Dialect* (Salford, 1812), p. 103.

44. Fulneck Elders Conference 12 October 1802, quoted in Ruth Strong 'Pudsey Fare', *Old West Riding* Vol. 6, No. 1 Summer 1986, p. 32.

45. John Travis, *Notes Historical and Biographical mainly of Todmorden and District* (Rochdale, 1896), p. 28.

46. R. W. S. Bishop, *My Moorland Patients* (London, 1922), p. 145.

47. 'Most cane molasses these days have some 50–55% sugars present but it is very likely that in the last century sugar recovery was less efficient and higher sugar contents were common in molasses.' Personal communication from Dr M. L. Burge, Tate and Lyle Sugars.

48. Leeds Mercury Weekly Supplement, Local Notes and Queries, 13 December 1884.

49. Frank Peel, *Spen Valley Past and Present* (Heckmondwike, 1893), p. 229.
50. Brears, p. 86.
51. J. Hartley, *The Clock Almanack* (1893), p. 57; (1879), p. 25.
52. Leeds Mercury Supplement, 3rd June 1899.
53. John Kirkland, *The Modern Baker* (London, 1911), Vol. 3, p. 451; Hartley, *The Clock Almanack* (1877), p. 25.
54. The making of parkin alone could account for the sales figures of Tate and Lyle syrups and treacles, which continue to be heaviest in Scotland and the north. Northern oatmeal sales are typified by those of Lodges, a small chain of village supermarkets in the Huddersfield area: their average weekly sales of oatmeal (500 gm pack) are 100 per week, but during the three weeks before and the week of November 5th these rise to 3,600.

I am grateful for information given by Michael Bacon, John Smurthwaite and Edward Law.

7.

A North Yorkshire Recipe Book

PETER BREARS

The history of a manuscript recipe book is often quite difficult to determine. When Mrs D. Stead of York generously loaned me her thick leather-bound volume, she had no knowledge of its past, the only clues being the watermark 'E & S 1810' on many of the pages and the inscription 'G. Healey, Middleton Tyas' inside the front cover. The recipes, meanwhile, both from their calligraphy and their content, suggested a late eighteenth- or early nineteenth-century date.

The Family

Entries in the county directories soon confirmed that George Healey had lived during the second quarter of the nineteenth century in the North Yorkshire village of Middleton Tyas. This small settlement lies just to the east of the Great North Road, the A1, at Scotch Corner, some seven miles south of Darlington. Further information gathered from the parish registers, census returns and local histories then allowed a much fuller picture to be built up.

Born in Yorkshire around 1791, George Healey had joined the North York Militia early in the Napoleonic wars, being promoted as lieutenant in 1803, captain in 1806, and major in 1814.[1] During this period he followed his regiment to Harwich, Newry, etc., enjoying the company of his fellow officers in the mess. It is recorded that in 1815, for example, Captain Johnson bet him and Captain Shafto each two bottles of wine that Miss . . . (a relative of a brother officer?) was 'not a Quean (whore)'. Major Healey won his bet, but left no clues as to how he obtained his evidence! Throughout this time he probably

22.
Middleton Lodge,
home of Elizabeth
Healey from 1784 to
1828.

built up a close friendship with two members of the Hartley family; Francis Hartley (1777–1820) who served as a captain in the regiment from 1803, and his brother, George (1780–1841), major in the North York Cavalry.

Their home was at Middleton Tyas, where they were among the major landowners, their wealth being gained from the discovery of copper ore in one of their limestone quarries in the 1730s. From this time through to the 1780s the copper mines proved extremely profitable, enabling the family to erect Middleton Lodge as their family home. Reputedly built to the designs of John Carr of York in 1779, this was the major house in the village, its elegant pedimented five-bay façade and Tuscan doorway all being constructed in finely-cut stonework.[2]

It was probably through their activities in the militia that George Healey first met Captain Francis' and Major George's younger sister, Elizabeth. The daughter of Leonard and Jane Hartley of Middleton Lodge, she had been baptised at St Michael's parish church on March 17th, 1784. It was here too that, as the registers record, 'George Healey of Stokesley in the Diocese of York [married] Elizabeth Hartley of this parish' on May 10th, 1825. The witnesses included her bachelor brother Major George, now head of the family, and Watson Martin and Hannah Jefferson, these presumably being personal friends. The couple appear to have moved in with George Hartley at Middleton Lodge, for, after only three years of married life, the parish records record the burial of Mrs Elizabeth Healey 'of Middleton Lodge' on September 5th, 1828, at the age of forty-four.

Major George Healey and Major George Hartley continued a close friendship through their military interests. On August 15th, 1831, for example, they both took part in an impressive review on Richmond racecourse following an intensive period of twenty-eight days training. First Major Healey drilled his 500 men, after which they were joined by Major Hartley's 200 cavalrymen. A similar order was maintained during the evening's festivities, Major Healey's officers first entertaining the cavalry officers to an excellent dinner, after which Major Hartley's officers gave a grand ball for Major Healey's infantry and their combined guests.

Within a few years George Healey had remarried and set up a new home at West Hall, the stylish early eighteenth-century residence on the main street of Middleton Tyas, which had been the home of the late Captain Francis Hartley. Although the registers record the burial of 'Laura Mildred Healey, daughter of Anna Mildred and George Healey, Major in the North York' on April 27th, 1835, the couple appear to have had no other children. George continued his interest in the militia, being promoted Lieutenant Colonel of the North York, Richmond (Rifles) in August, 1852. By the mid-1850s, the Healeys had removed from West Hall to Morris Grange, Moulton, a village a mile and a half south of Middleton Tyas. It was here that George died and Anna passed her widowhood.

Although the signature of 'G. Healey' shows that the recipe book was once his property, it does not provide any evidence as to who actually compiled it, particularly since he is extremely unlikely to have had any concern with culinary affairs. Most probably it was written by his first wife, Elizabeth, or his second wife, Anna.

The arguments for this being Elizabeth Hartley's book are particularly strong. The 1810 watermark, for example, could suggest that it had been purchased when she was in her late twenties and was beginning to take over the household management of Middleton Lodge from her ageing widowed mother, who died in 1815. Members of her family also prominently figure as donors of recipes, the most obvious being her mother, Mrs Leonard Hartley. Her mother's family, the Bucktons, also made their contributions, as did her paternal aunt, Margaret Hartley, who had died in 1802. The recipes of the Charge family come from the marriage of her elder sister Jane (1773–1840) to Thomas Charge of Barton Hall, Barton St Mary's, two miles north of Middleton Tyas, lieutenant in the militia. Those from the Campbells, meanwhile, come from the marriage of her elder sister, Mary (1786–1855), to Archibald Campbell.

Further recipes come from friends in the neighbourhood, such as the Halls, the Harrisons and the Olivers, all farmers in the village, or ladies with private means such as Mrs Motley, Miss St A. Ward of nearby Moulton Manor House or Lady Milbanke of Thorpe Perrow. Considering the military interests of Elizabeth's family, it is not surprising to find that a number of other recipes come from the families of officers serving in the North York Militia. These include Lieutenant Charles Allen, Colonel Sheldon Cradock, M.P. of Hartforth Hall, Lieutenant-Colonel William Hale, Captain P. Hammond and probably Ensign Robert or Lieutenant Joseph Nicholson.

In complete contrast, there is very little evidence to suggest that Anna Healey added to this volume, unless she was responsible for a number of recipes in a later hand, some of which are dated to the later 1860s. In these circumstances it would appear that this recipe book was compiled between *c.*1810 and 1828 by Elizabeth Healey née Hartley of Middleton Lodge, Middleton Tyas, with some of the recipes being handed down from earlier members of her family.

If Elizabeth Healey were to return to Middleton Tyas today, she would find a remarkable number of things just as she left them over 160 years ago. Most of the same houses still line the long village street, and the road leading northwards to Middleton Lodge still passes through rich arable enclosed within quickthorn hedges. Down the drive, across the ha-ha, and round to the left, the extensive kitchen garden that supplied all her fruit and vegetables still stands within its rose-pink brick wall, its northern face being heated by means of a stove and long horizontal flues. If she should decide to enter the Lodge through its service wing, she would find the brew-house half complete, the furnace and the steps leading up to the copper standing against its eastern wall. The drying-room next door has its cast-iron range, its ironing benches, and the ratchetted winch, roller and pulleys by which the huge clothes rack could be hoisted up to the ceiling all perfectly intact. Just along the corridor she would recognise the door with the perforated zinc gauze in its upper panels as the entrance to the game larder. Inside, the high beams with their neat rows of wrought-iron hooks would have supported dozens of brace of hanging pheasants, hares, rabbits and other game and the shelves and meat-safes lining the walls would have held their store of mutton and beef, poultry, etc. Continuing round a dog-leg in the passage, and through a door to the right would bring her into her scullery, where one wall has its central iron range (now Victorian) flanked by two iron boilers set in masonry furnaces, their tops having close-fitting wooden doors and flues ventilating into the chimney stack to carry away their steam and cooking smells. One was probably used for laundry, while

Middleton Tyas and Middleton Lodge

23.
The larder has metal gauze in its window and door, and was divided by a pierced screen so that it always remained cool and well-ventilated.

the other could boil vegetables and puddings, or scald chickens ready for the kitchen. Next, the kitchen itself is high, well-lit and spacious. Its southern half was partitioned off and modernised in the 1950s, but the end wall still shows traces of three elliptically-arched fireplace recesses, the central one, with its deep ashpit, having presumably been occupied by a roasting range flanked by a hotplate at

24.
In the scullery the late eighteenth century oval boiler is divided into two, so that two distinct foods may be cooker separately.

one side and hot-cupboards on the other. The northern end of the kitchen is still virtually as Elizabeth left it, with dry-brushed stone-colour paint up to door-head height, and whitewash above. An enormous pine dresser takes up most of the north wall, with a magnificent white marble mortar set within a massive sandstone plinth standing at one end. Employing a heavy pestle, Elizabeth must have regularly used this most luxurious of eighteenth-century food-processors to reduce her cooked meats, her lemon-peels, etc. to perfectly smooth pastes. A spit-rack against the west wall completes the furnishing of this room.

From the kitchen, the domestic staff would have carried the food along the broad corridor, past the pantry, the housekeeper's room and the butler's pantry, into the very heart of the house. Here Elizabeth would have welcomed her guests from the porch, through the rectangular entrance hall, and into the staircase hall, one of Carr's minor masterpieces. Elliptical in plan, and rising through the full height of the house, this is a room of great elegance and beauty. Light floods in from the glazed centre of its sumptuous plasterwork dome, picking out the crisp, classical detail of its pedimented doorways. From the cantilevered gallery which gives access to the first-floor rooms a staircase sweeps down to the ground floor in the most gracious manner. When dinner was ready, she would have proceeded with family and guests through into the adjoining dining-room. Here the doorway from the hall is flanked by two deep half-round niches, their domed heads being enriched with fine plasterwork. Down the centre of the room extended the long table, with a sideboard to the left and the fireplace to the right, the rounded wall at the far end being pierced by the three large sash windows of one of Carr's characteristic semi-hexagonal bays. It would have been in these elegant surroundings that all Elizabeth's fine recipes would have achieved the success they undoubtedly deserved. Following the etiquette of the day, she presumably would have left the gentlemen to their port (and talk of militia affairs past, present, and future) at the end of the meal, retiring with the other ladies to her splendid drawing room. Here conversation would naturally turn to culinary affairs, and notes would be taken of the visitor's favourite recipes, which could then be tried out at some future dinner party. It is these recipes which form the content of Elizabeth Healey's extensive manuscript recipe book.

25.
The mortar in the kitchen at Middleton Lodge was probably used by Elizabeth Healey for pounding her cooked meats, lemon peels, etc. into the smoothest pastes.

Having given the volume a reasonably firm provenance, it is now possible to move on to consider its contents in greater detail, particularly with regard to the ways in which they record the cooking traditions of North Yorkshire's prosperous farmers and gentry during the opening years of the nineteenth century.

'In the days of Good Queen Elizabeth', wrote Campbell,

The Origins of The Recipes in the Book

195

'mighty Roast Beef was the Englishman's Food, Our Cookery was plain and simple as our Manners, it was not then a Science or Mistery, and required no Conjunction to please the Palates of our greatest Men. But we have of late Years refined ourselves out of that simple Taste . . .'[3] This process of refinement had started in Queen Elizabeth's court where the wives of the courtiers and the young upwardly-progressive country gentry found their way into the all-male preserve of the Royal kitchens, and there began to extract the recipes for the finest dishes in the land. Cookery soon became an extremely popular and important accomplishment for any lady of quality. She would have frequent need to display her skills when entertaining her family, her friends, and (as with today's company wives) those who could further her husband's career; and so every opportunity was taken to note down good recipes from every available source. In addition to those which she might obtain through personal contacts, a splendid supply was soon being provided by the London publishers, including *A Proper Newe Book of Cokerye* of *c.*1572; J. Partridge's *The Widowes Treasure* of 1585; *The Good Hous-wives Treasurie* of 1588; A.W.'s *Book of Cookrye Very necessary for all such as delight therein* of 1584 with other later editions; Thomas Dawson's *The Good Huswifes Jewell* of 1596, and its anonymous *Second Part* of 1597.

By these means a wide-ranging but still very distinctive style of fine cookery had become firmly established within the households of the nobility and gentry by the close of the sixteenth century. Its richly-flavoured meat dishes, its excellent bakery, and its amazingly succulent and ornamental confectionery all continued to develop over the next hundred years, as is testified by the content of the numerous family recipe books and printed cookery books which still survive from this period. Tastes then began to change, however, particularly as a result of an increasing French influence. While these developments were taking place, the Elizabethan cookery tradition began to work its way down the social scale, from the nobility to the gentry, and so on to the merchants, the clergy, and prosperous farming families such as the Healeys of Middleton Tyas. Most of the 'traditional' cookery of the English regions can be traced back to this source, being adapted as necessary to meet varying local circumstances.

The chief interest of the Healey cookery book lies in the evidence it provides for the continuity of late sixteenth- and early seventeenth-century recipes through to the early nineteenth century. Unlike many manuscript recipe books of this period, it owes comparatively little to printed sources, but instead gathers its content entirely from the family's personal acquaintances living within the area of North Yorkshire adjoining the border with County Durham. Although this aspect is very difficult to define, most of the recipes give the impression that they have been modified or 'polished' by generations of cooks, the practicality and relative simplicity of the techniques, the lack of lavish spicing, and the uniform good quality of the final results all pointing in this direction.

Most of the recipes have long and well-established pedigrees. The calfs foot pie is very similar to A.W.'s 1584 instructions 'To bake pyes of calves feet', for example, while the mutton cutlets follow the Elizabethan practice of slowly frying mutton steaks with herbs over a gentle heat, as described in *The Second Part of the Good Huswifes Jewell* of 1597. Similarly the method of cooking meat within a sealed jar immersed in a pot of boiling water described in 'to stew beef' follows late sixteenth-century practice. The Scotch collops, meanwhile, thin stir-fried slices of veal or mutton, their juices thickened into a rich sauce, go back to the early seventeenth century at least. After the battle of Worcester, for example, even Charles II was sufficiently familiar with this dish to 'cut some of it [mutton] into Collops . . . call for a Frying-pan and butter, and fry the collops himself.'[4] The appearance of a recipe for Yorkshire

Christmas Pie in the Healey recipe book is of particular interest, since it is one of the very few manuscript versions extant for this gargantuan dish of tongue, chickens, hare and goose, traditionally made each year on December 26th, St Stephen's day. In complete contrast to these extremely well-established dishes, there are instructions for making curry powder (largely turmeric), and for using it to produce chicken curry. This spicy Indian dish had been growing in popularity throughout the late eighteenth century, but it is interesting to find it here in an otherwise entirely English context.

The puddings described in the recipe book are all excellent, but they show how the English pudding had progressed through a number of stages over the previous two hundred years. In the early seventeenth century most puddings had been made of flavoured meats and cereals enclosed within a sheep's stomach, or gut, or even a breast of veal, a carp, or a tench. From this time, however, pudding cloths came into general use, enabling the ingredients to be simply tied up and plunged into boiling water for the requisite period, as in the plum pudding recipe. It was then found that lighter puddings were produced if they were placed in a pottery basin, tied down beneath a pudding cloth and steamed over boiling water, as demonstrated by the brown bread and pease puddings seen here. As a further improvement, the puddings were poured into greased dishes and baked in the oven as pudding pies. These became much more common once cast-iron ranges with hot-air ovens came into general use during the late eighteenth and early nineteenth centuries. They are represented in this recipe book by cheese, potato and carrot puddings, and many other varieties.

The cold desserts such as custards, jellies, blancmanges, preserved fruits and flowers, and various cream-based dishes, all owe their origins to the elaborate banqueting-stuffs served as the last course at magnificent sixteenth and seventeenth century entertainments. The stone cream, thickened with isinglass, has close similarities to the early steeple creams, but is further enriched with preserved apricots and lemon juice. The syllabub, meanwhile, although visually resembling the rich, smooth and delicate flavour of its predecessors, is quite a poor affair, being a mere cream and egg-white froth spooned on top of red or white wine. A remarkable survival of the thick quince *marmelado* imported from Portugal in the fifteenth century for medicinal and dessert use is provided by the recipe for 'apple paste'.[5] This comprises a solid block of dark-red apple conserve studded with split almonds and surrounded by a border of yellow custard.

Other desserts are far more modern in character. The 'truffle of apples' corresponds closely to the trifle published in John Farley's *The London Art of Cookery* of 1783, with the notable differences that it was contained within a wall of boiled rice, and substituted stewed apples for the earlier ratafias. Italian creams, made by curdling thick sweet cream with lemon juice and white wine, were also of quite recent introduction, the necessary pierced creamware moulds being made in the industrial potteries of West Yorkshire.

As with most cookery books of this period, there are various recipes for drinks, ranging from thirst-quenching fruit vinegars and lemonades for hot summer days to beers, mead, punch and country wines. The latter include 'Frontineack', an English substitute for the muscat wines of Frontignan imported from the early seventeenth century, if not earlier, and 'Rattafee', a liqueur flavoured with almonds, apricot or peach kernels popular since Stuart times.

The bakery includes the usual range of egg-raised cakes similar to those of the seventeenth century. The bride cake is clearly descended from the earlier 'great cake', for example, while the seed cake, shortcake, pepper cake and gingerbread all compare very closely with their predecessors. By this time, however, cracknels were being baked on iron sheets in the oven, without having a preliminary boiling,

26.
In the quiet rural churchyard of Middleton Tyas, Elizabeth Healey now lies beneath this elegant tomb amid her Hartley relations.

the recently-introduced iron ovens also being ideal for baking both sweet biscuits and the crisp water biscuits which made an ideal accompaniment to cheese.

Although the Healey manuscript extends to over 250 pages, it is hoped that the following selection of thirty-three recipes will enable the reader to gain an accurate impression of some of North Yorkshire's finest traditional cookery. In each example the quantities and methods have been revised for present-day use, but the resulting dish is intended to reproduce the original as closely as possible. Do try them – they really do repay the effort involved in their preparation.

Notes and References

1. For details of George Healey's military activities, see R. B. Turton, *The History of the North York Militia* (Stockton-on-Tees, 1973), pp. 116–20; 122; 184.
2. T. R. Hornshaw, *Copper-mining at Middleton Tyas* (North Yorkshire County Record Office Publications no. 6, Northallerton, 1975). The Hartley pedigree appears on pp. 18–19.
3. R. Campbell, *The London Tradesman* (London, 1747), p. 276.
4. T. Blount, *Boscobel* (London, 1660), p. 35.
5. C. A. Wilson, *The Book of Marmalade* (London, 1985), p. 30–34.

A North Yorkshire Recipe Book

To Stew Beef   Mrs L. Hartley

*Cut your beef as for a pye, put it into a Jar with pepper and salt, a layer of
Beef then Onions till your Jar is as full as you like, put a tea cup of water
to it, tie it close down with a plate, so that the steam cannot get out, set it
in a kettle of water which must be kept boiling all the time, and as the
water wastes away, fill your pan up. 2 or 3 lb. of Beef will take 3 hours
Stewing, you may have Carrots, Turnips & small Onions ready boil'd to
lay on your Beef. Serve it in a Tureen or deep Dish.*

> 2 lb (900g) braising steak
> 2 lb (900g) onions, peeled, halved, and sliced
> 1 lb (450g) each of carrots, turnips and quartered onions prepared
>   for boiling
> 1 cup (200ml) water

Cube the beef and place in layers with the onions in a deep casserole,
seasoning it to taste as the vessel is filled. Pour in the water, seal the
top with kitchen foil, and bake for 3 hours at gas mark 3, 325°F (170°C0.
After 2½ hours put the remaining vegetables in a pan and simmer for
about 15 minutes or until cooked.

   To serve, either drain the vegetables and tip them on top of the meat
in the casserole, or put the meat into a large tureen and cover with the
vegetables.

Scotch Collops White   Mrs L. Hartley

*Cut them of the thick part of a leg of Mutton the size and thickness of a
crown piece, put a lump of butter into a tossing pan & set over a slow fire
or it will discolour your Collops. before the pan is hot lay the Collops in
& keep turning them over till you see the butter is turned to thick white
gravy. put your Collops & gravy into a pot & set them upon the hearth to
keep warm. put cold butter again into your pan every time you fill it &
fry them as above & so continue till you have finished. When you have
fried them pour the gravy from them into your pan with a teaspoonful of
Lemon Pickle, Mushroom Catchup, Caper Liquor, beaten Mace, Chyan
pepper & salt. Thicken with flour & butter. when it has boiled five
minutes put in the yolks of 2 eggs well beat and mixed with a tea cup full
of thick cream, keep shaking the pan over the fire till your gravy looks of
a fine thickness, then put in your collops and shake them. when they are
quite hot put them on your dish with force meat Balls. strew over them
pickled Mushrooms, garnish with Barberries & Kidney Beans.*

> 1 lb (450g) lean leg or lamb or mutton
> 3 oz (75g) butter
> 1 tbs (15 ml) flour
> ½ tsp (2.5 ml) lemon pickle
> 2 tbs (30 ml) mushroom ketchup
> pinch of mace and of Cayenne pepper
> yolk of one egg
> ⅓ pt (200 ml) single cream

Slice the meat as thinly as possible, and gently fry in batches in two ounces of the butter, tipping the meat and gravy into a second pan placed on a low heat until all the meat is cooked. Melt the remaining butter and flour in the first pan and make a roux, mix in the pickle, ketchup and spices, and the gravy drained from the meat and cook gently for 5 minutes. Add the egg beaten into the cream and cook, stirring until smooth and thick before adding the meat and heating through.

Mutton Cutlets   Mrs Hartley

Take steaks of Mutton from the best end of the neck, cut the bones short & scrape the ends of the bones clean from the meat & take part of the fat off them. rub your steaks over with pepper, Salt, Thyme, & Sweet Marjoram, fry them, then have some cream. Turnips put in the middle of your Dish with some good Gravy, lay the steaks round it. The brown Gravy would be good for this Dish

> 6 small mutton steaks
> ½ pt (275 ml) single cream
> pepper, salt, ground thyme and marjoram
> 2 lb (900g) turnips
> 2 oz (50g) butter

Boil the turnips in salted water for 20–30 minutes until tender, drain, and mash with a little of the butter and cream. Meanwhile, dust the steaks with the pepper, salt and herbs, and gently fry in the butter, adding the cream to the pan to make a thick sauce just before serving. Make the turnips into a shallow cone on a hot plate, arrange the steaks around the sides, and coat with the sauce from the frying pan.

Christmas or Yorkshire Raised Pie   Mrs Wharton

The Crust
1 Peck of fine Flour, Knead it with suet, which must be well boiled. Make the whole into a very stiff paste. Bake it 6 hours.

Veal forcemeat to line the Pie
2 oz of lean veal, 2 oz of Beef Suet, 2 oz of bread crumbs. chop fine a little parsley, Lemon peel & sweet herbs & onions. pound in a Mortar. break in the Yoke and White of an egg. Mix it well together & season with pepper & salt. The Goose, Hare, Chickens, are to be boned before putting in & stuffed one into another & salted tongue as the Centre.

Savoury Jelly for the top
Spread slices of lean beef & ham in a stewpan with a turnip, Carrot, Celery, 3 or 4 onions & sweet herbs. Cover it & let it stew over a slow fire till it is a good brown. then put water in & let it boil. Strain it well & make it strong to Jelly. When cold take off the fat. Add salt & tarragon Vinegar to your taste, clear with white of eggs & run thro' a Jelly bag.

A North Yorkshire Recipe Book

Currie Powder

¾ lb Turmeric
¼ lb black Pepper
1 oz cardamom seeds
2 oz Cummin seed
2 oz coriander seed
½ oz Ginger

To be well pounded & mixed together by a Chemist

Receipt for a Curry   Mrs Darville

For one chicken take 4 teaspoonfuls of curry powder & one teaspoonful of Turmarick, put it into a Mortar with a little water & Clove of Garlic & beat it well, then rub it well over each piece of the Chicken & throw in some Salt & a little more water, then take a Stew pan, put a large piece of butter into it & hold it over the fire till the butter is melted (take care not to burn it) then cut the Onion & throw the Chicken into the butter, & fry it till thoroughly done. Before you Dish it add a little lemon Juice.

1 chicken
1 clove of garlic, crushed
1 large English onion
3 oz (75g) butter
juice of ½ lemon

½ tsp (2.5 ml) salt
1 tbs (15 ml) turmeric
1 tsp (5 ml) black pepper
large pinch each of ground
cardamom, cummin, corriander
& ginger

Bone the chicken, cut into pieces as if for stewing, and rub with the garlic, salt and spices mixed into a paste with a little water. Melt the butter in a thick-bottomed pan, put in the onion and chicken, and gently stir-fry until thoroughly cooked. Serve with boiled rice.

Cheese Pudding   Mrs L. Hartley

½ a lb of potatoes beaten fine, ¼ of a lb of Cheese scraped fine, 3 oz of fresh butter, 3 Eggs & a little Cream cold, pepper, & salt, mix it well together, & bake it ¾ of an hour.

8 oz (225g) potatoes, boiled and mashed
4 oz (100g) finely grated cheese
3 oz (75g) butter
3 eggs
Pepper and salt to taste

Work the butter into the potatoes, then the cheese and eggs, beating the mixture until quite smooth. Alternatively all the ingredients may be blended in a food processor. Pour into a greased 2pt. souffle dish and bake at gas mark 2, 300°F (150°C) for 45 minutes. Serve immediately. This potato-based cheese souffle is really excellent.

Potatoe Pudding   Mrs L. Hartley

*Boil potatoes & bruize them very fine, take a lb. & put to them ½ a lb of
butter, 6 oz of loaf Sugar finely powder'd, beat 8 Eggs together, then the
sugar & butter, just before you put it in the oven, put to it the juice of a
large lemon & grate the out rind into it, mix it well and bake in a quick
oven.*

    8 oz (225g) potatoes, boiled and mashed
    4 oz (100g) butter
    3 oz (75g) sugar
    3 eggs
    juice & grated rind of half a lemon.

Work the butter into the potatoes, then the beaten eggs and sugar,
beating the mixture until perfectly smooth. Alternatively all the
ingredients except the lemon may be blended together in a food processor.
Stir in the lemon juice and rind just before pouring the mixture into a
greased 2 pt. souffle dish and baking at gas mark 2, 300°F (150°C) for
45 minutes. Serve immediately. Another excellent pudding.

Scallop Potatoes   Mrs Penrose

*Take cold boiled Potatoes, grate them fine & put a little Salt in them, &
cream, put them in a Scallop whole, press them down, then turn them
out & set them before the fire to brown, with a little butter on the top.*

Today the potatoes can be cooked beneath a grill at a medium heat.

Pease Pudding   Mrs Morley

*Boil a pint of Pease till tender, then pulp them through a Sieve and beat
them, add three Eggs two tablespoonfuls of Cream and a small piece of
butter, and a little Salt, these ingredients must be all beat together. put
into a Mould, and boil an hour.*

    1 lb (450g) boiled peas or drained contents of a 539g can
    3 small eggs
    2 tbs (30 ml) cream
    ½ tsp (5 ml) salt
    ½ oz (15g) butter

Blend all the ingredients together until smooth, then pour into a buttered
1½ pt (700 ml) pudding basin, seal tightly with cooking foil and steam in
a covered pan of boiling water for an hour before turning out on a
warmed plate. Mint sauce makes a good accompaniment.

Carrot Pudding

*Grate raw Carrots & put as much more grated bread as Carrot, with a
Nutmeg, 8 Eggs, leave out 2 whites ¼ of a lb of Butter. Sugar to your
taste, bake it.*

8 oz (225g) fresh bread crumbs
8 oz (225g) finely grated carrot
4 eggs
3 oz (75g) butter
3 oz (75g) sugar
½ tsp (2.5 ml) grated nutmeg

Mix together the dry ingredients, then add the melted butter and the beaten eggs, working the mixture thoroughly before placing in a 2 pt. ovenproof dish and baking at gas mark 3, 325°F (170°C) for an hour.

Brown Bread Pudding   Mrs L. Hartley

Ten ounces of Brown Bread grated fine, the same quantity of Suit shred, seven Eggs, two Tablespoonfuls of Brandy, a little Mace, & Nutmeg, four Tablespoonfuls of Moist Sugar, the juice of half a Lemon, a little of the Peel shred small, preserved Orange cut thin as you like, this quantity will take four hours Boiling — Your Mold must be full & put the Pudding into Cold Water

4 oz (100g) wholemeal breadcrumbs   7 eggs, beaten
4 oz (100g) suet   1 tbs (15 ml) brandy
2 tbs (30 ml) moist brown sugar   ¼ juice of a lemon
1 oz (25g) chopped candied peel

Mix all the ingredients, pour into a 1½ pt (1 litre) bowl, tightly cover with cooking foil, and steam for two hours.

Stone Cream   Miss M. A. Lloyd

Squeeze the juice of a large lemon into a Dish, & grate the rind, then lay upon it preserv'd apricots or Plums, having ready a pint of Cream & half an Oz of Isinglass dissolved in it, sweeten it & let it go nearly cold before you pour it on the Sweetmeats. garnish the top of it with colou'd Sugar or Sweetmeats.

1 pt (275 ml) double cream
2 tbs (30 ml) caster sugar
1 small tin apricot halves, drained
1 lemon
2 tsp (10 ml) gelatine

Grate the lemon and put into a shallow bowl with the strained juice. Arrange the apricots on top. Melt the gelatine in 2 tbs (30 ml) boiling water in a cup, and stand in boiling water for a few minutes until completely dissolved. Gently beat the sugar into the cream, then mix in the gelatine and pour over the apricots and lemon juice in the bowl. Leave in a cool place for a few hours to produce a smooth, delicious lemon-flavoured dessert. A layer of sieved apricot jam or a sprinkling of sugar may be used to finish this dish.

Italian Cream   *Mrs W. Hall*

A pint of thick cream & the juice and rinds of 2 lemons, 4 tablespoonfuls of white Wine, with sugar to your taste, these ingredients put into a bowl & work it for ½ an hour then put it into a tin mould that has holes in it, a thin muslin or gauze must be laid in the mould to secure the cheese.

> 1 pt (575 ml) double cream
> juice and grated rind of 2 lemons
> 4 tbs (60 ml) white wine
> 4 tbs (60 ml) sugar

This rich dessert was originally made in fine earthenware moulds which incorporated numerous tiny holes through which the whey could drain away. To make Italian cheese today, start by drilling a pint-sized plastic jelly mould with a regular pattern of 1/16 inch holes. Line this with fine muslin, and pour in the above ingredients beaten together for half an hour. Leave the mould to drain in a cold place for at least twelve hours, then turn out onto a plate and carefully remove the muslin.

To make a Syllabub   *Mrs L. Hartley*

Take a quart of thick cream, whites of 3 Eggs. whip it to a froth, as it rises, put it on a coarse sieve to drain, then take either Red wine or white put it in Glasses, lay froth at the top, or you may put it over sweetmeats in a Glass Bason.

> 7 fl oz (200 ml) whipping cream
> white of one egg
> 2 glasses (280 ml) red or white wine

Whip the cream and egg-white together until thick and carefully spoon over the wine previously distributed between six balloon wine-glasses. Stand in a cool place for at least an hour before serving.

Truffle of Apples   *Mrs Oliver*

Take some common Rice creed with lemon peel or Cinnamon, make it up like a standing pie on the dish you mean to send it to the table on, then put coddled apples at the Bottom & fill it with thick Custard. Whipped cream is an addition.

> 8 oz (225g) pudding rice   1 pt (575 ml) custard
> 6 eating apples (e.g. Cox's Pippins)   ½ pt (275 ml) whipped cream
> 4 oz (125g) sugar
> peel of one lemon or 1 stick cinnamon

Gently simmer the rice and either the lemon peel or the cinnamon in 2 pts (1.1 litre) water in a covered pan for some 30–40 minutes, stirring continuously towards the end until it is very stiff. Remove the peel or cinnamon, allow to cool, and model as a 2–3 inch (50–70 cm) high wall just inside the rim of a large dinner plate. Meanwhile peel and core the apples and simmer with their peels and the sugar for some 10–15 minutes, until tender. Drain the apples, place within the rice wall and cover with the warm custard before leaving them to cool. Finally top with the whipped cream and serve.

Apple Paste

Pare & core some apples, put them into a Stew-pan, Stew them till quite tender, then rub them thro 'a Sieve, add a lb. of loaf Sugar (first boiling it with a little water to a candy height) add 1 lb of the Apple pulp to the Sugar mixing it smooth. Boil it half an hour, stir it all the time, add to it the rind & juice of a lemon, put it in a mould, turn it out when quite cold into a dish, pour Custard round it & stick sliced Almons in it.

    4 apples (e.g. Cox's Pippins)
    1 lemon
    12 oz (350g) sugar
    ¾ pt (425 ml) custard
    split blanched almonds for decoration

Peel, core and chop the apples, put in a pan with the grated peel of the lemon and very little water. Allow to cook to a soft pulp, then rub through a sieve, weigh, add its weight of sugar, the juice of the lemon, and cook for half an hour, during which time it will thicken and darken in colour. Rub the inside of a one-pint (550 ml) basin with butter, and pour in the paste before standing in a cool place for a few hours until thoroughly set. Ease the paste away from the sides of the basin with a knife and turn out into a deep dish, using the knife to smooth any rough areas. Pour the custard around the sides, stud the paste with sliced blanched almonds, and allow to cool before serving.

Plum Pudding

1 lb of Suet not very small cut, ½ a lb of flour, ¾ of a lb of Currants, ½ a lb of Raisins, stoned & cut, mix all these together with 4 Eggs, a little Salt, nutmeg & Ginger, beat your Eggs well, & if they will not wet the ingredients so as to make it a stiff paste, take as much new Milk as will do it, tie it up very tight, put it into cold water, it will take 4 hours boiling. half this quantity is a good sized pudding. if boil'd in a Mould you must mind it is quite full or your pudding will be spoilt

4 oz (100g) suet	4 oz (100g) raisins
4 oz (100g) flour	1 tsp (5 ml) each of ground
6 oz (175g) currants	ginger & grated nutmeg
2 eggs, lightly beaten	½ pt (275 ml) milk

Mix together the dry ingredients, make a well in the centre, pour in the eggs and gradually stir in, adding sufficient milk little by little to make a stiff paste. Turn the mixture into a moistened and floured cloth, tie it tightly, place in a pan of cold water, bring to the boil and continue boiling for 3½ hours.

Alternatively, place in a greased 2 pt (1 litre) basin, cover with cling wrap, pierce twice, and microwave at full power for nine minutes, then leave to stand for a further ten minutes before turning out.

Lemonade *Mrs Hogg*

To the rinds of 10 lemons & 4 Seville Oranges pared very thin, put a pound of loaf Sugar & 2 quarts of Spring water boiling hot, stir it to dissolve the sugar, let it stand one day, covering it close, then squeeze into it the juice of the 10 lemons & 4 Seville Oranges, add to it a pint of white wine. Boil a pint of new milk & pour it on boiling hot upon the ingredients, when cold run it through a Calico Bag. China Oranges will do.

10 lemons	1 lb (450g) sugar
4 Seville oranges	1 pt (.5 litres) white wine
4 pt (2.3 litres) water	1 pt (.5 litres) milk

Follow the above instructions to produce a beautifully smooth, fine lemonade, with surprisingly good thirst-quenching properties.

Raspberry Vinegar *Mrs Hall Stephen*

Put a pint of white wine vinegar in a quart of Raspberryes, cover it close & let it stand 24 hours, then strain it through a Sieve, put to that Liquor another quart of Raspberries, let it remain on it 24 hours more, strain it 1 lb of good Sugar, set it on the fire in a large sauce pan & boil it 20 minutes. when cold Bottle it.

1 pt (0.5 litres) white wine vinegar
1 lb (450g) raspberries (fresh or frozen)
1 lb (450g) sugar

Soak the raspberries in the vinegar for 24 hours before straining off all the liquor through a muslin. Add the sugar and simmer for 20 minutes before pouring into sterilised bottles and sealing closely. Dilute to taste for a pleasantly sharp and refreshing drink, or try neat on pancakes.

Shrub *Mrs M. Hartley*

To 4 Gallons of Rum or Brandy, put 5 pints of Orange juice & 4 lb and a half of Loaf Sugar, put these into an open Vessel of pot, stirring it every day for a week, then let it stand till it is fine, run the thick through a flannel Bag, Bottle it, the Spirit & Sugar must be first mixed together, then put it to the juice.

½ pt (275 ml) rum or brandy	1 oz (25g) sugar
3 tbs (50 ml) fresh orange juice	

Put the spirit and sugar into a bottle and shake until dissolved, add the orange juice, cork, and shake daily for a week. Allow to rest in a cool place until clear, pass through a coffee filter paper, and bottle for use.

A North Yorkshire Recipe Book

Toast and Ale 1868

3 pints of ale, 1 nutmeg grated, 1 tea spoonful grated ginger, sweeten to taste with raw sugar, put all in a jug, place it near the fire for half an hour till new milk warm, then add a few pieces of bread well toasted & a large sized glass of sherry.

1 pt (575 ml) strong brown ale	¼ tsp (1.5 ml) ground ginger
2 tbs (30 ml) sugar	1 tbs (1.5 ml) sherry
½ tsp (2.5 ml) ground nutmeg	1 slice well-done toast

Follow the instructions above.

Bride's Cake   Mrs Angles

1 lb of Raisins stoned, 3¼ lb of Currants, 3¼ of a lb of Almonds blanched & cut long ways, 1¼ lb of Flour, 1¼ lb of Butter, 1 lb of Sugar pounded & sifted, 14 Eggs well whisked, 1 nutmeg, ½ an Oz of Cinnamon & a piece of Mace well beaten, ½ a Gill of Brandy, ½ lb of Candied Orange, 3 Oz of Citron & a little rose water.

7 oz (200g) flour	2 tsp (10 ml) ground cinnamon
5 oz (150g) raisins	7 oz (200g) butter
1 lb (450g) currants	5 oz (150g) sugar
4 oz (100g) candied peel	4 eggs
4 oz (100g) flaked almonds	1 tbs (15 ml) rosewater
1 tsp (5 ml) ground mace	2 tbs (30 ml) brandy

Line a 10 inch (25 cm) cake tin with greaseproof paper, and tie a double layer of brown paper around the outside. Mix the sifted flour, spices, fruit and almonds together. In a separate bowl cream the butter and sugar until light and fluffy, then beat in the eggs a little at a time, followed by the rosewater and the brandy. Fold in half the flour and fruit, then fold in the rest, and spread evenly in the tin. Bake for 3 hours at gas mark 2, 300°F (150°C). As with many traditional fruit cakes, it is extremely dry when freshly baked, and so it should be left in an airtight tin or wrapped in cooking foil for some weeks before use. In many households it would have been pricked with a fine skewer and 'fed' with brandy to help it to mature.

A Cake   Mrs Gill

1 lb of flour well dried, 1 lb of Butter, 1 lb of Sugar beat fine, 10 Eggs leave out 4 whites, 2 Spoonfulls of Brandy, ¾ lb of Currants, mix your Butter & Sugar together, then your Eggs & flour, beat it one hour, put your Currants in just before you send it to the oven.

6 oz (175g) plain flour	4 oz (100g) currants
6 oz (175g) sugar	2 tsp (10 ml) brandy
3 eggs, less one white	

Cream the butter with the sugar until pale and fluffy, then add the eggs and brandy a little at a time, beating well after each addition. Fold in the flour, then the currants, and place the mixture in a 7 inch (18 cm) tin lined with greased greaseproof paper. Bake for about 1½ hours at gas mark 3, 325°F (170°C).

Ginger Bread   Mrs St A. Warde

1 lb of Treacle, ½ an Oz of Cloves, Do. of Cinnamon, 1 oz of Ginger, Do. of Carroway Seeds, & Do. Corriander seeds, beat all Spices & Seeds separately, & sift them apart, then set the treacle on the fire, put in a lb. of butter, then put in the Seeds & Spices, keeping it Stirring till all the butter be melted, let it simmer a little, & let it stand till cold, put in 2½ lb of flour & make it into small Nuts & bake them on tin plates in a quick Oven.

4 oz (100g) treacle	½ tsp (2.5 ml) each ground cloves &
4 oz (100g) sugar	cinnamon
4 oz (100g) butter	1 tsp (5 ml) each of ground ginger &
10 oz (275g) flour	caraway seeds

Place a saucepan on the scales and pour in the treacle, add the sugar, spices and butter, and heat gently, stirring continuously until the butter is completely melted, then allow the mixture to cool. Work in the sifted flour little by little to form a stiff dough. Knead it well, roll into balls the size of walnuts, place on greased baking sheets and bake at gas mark 2, 300°F (150°C0 for 20 minutes.

Very crisp when baked, these ginger nuts soon soften sufficiently to be eaten if left in the kitchen for a few days. Air-tight tins were not in general use when this recipe was written.

Sweet Biscuits   Mrs Pearse

1 lb of Flour well dried, 1 lb of Sugar sifted, 1 lb of Currants, 3 Eggs well beat & as much cold good milk as will mix & drop. not to rise.

4 oz (100g) plain flour	1 beaten egg
4 oz (100g) sugar	¼ pt (150 ml) milk
4 oz (100g) currants	

Mix the dry ingredients, make a hole in the middle and drop in the egg, gradually working it into the mixture with just sufficient milk to produce a soft dropping consistency. Spoon large walnut-sized piles of the mixture three inches (8 cm) apart on greased baking sheets, and bake for 20–30 minutes at gas mark 2, 300°F (150°C) until lightly coloured, just browning at the edges.

Biscuits   Mrs Hartley

2 lb of Flour, the white of an Egg, 4 oz of Butter, melt the Butter in new milk, about a gill, mix it into paste, roll it very thin & cut your Cakes with a Cup or a Saucer the size you like, prick them well with a Fork, work your paste half an hour, bake them in a moderate oven, not to be brown.

8 oz (225g) plain flour
1 oz (25g) butter
¼ pt (150 ml) milk

Heat the milk and butter until just melted, allow to cool a little, then pour into a hole formed in the flour, quickly work them together to form a warm dough, and continue kneading, flouring from time to time, for half an hour. By this time it will have become extremely smooth. Divide the dough into three, then roll each piece out to around 1/16 inch (.2 cm) in thickness, cut into 3 inch (8 cm) rounds, and prick each one extremely closely with a fork. Place on a baking sheet and bake for 10 minutes at gas mark 2, 300°F (150°C).

These very thin, crisp plain biscuits make a good accompaniment to cheese, or may be spread with home-made jams or jellies.

To pot Beef or Mutton   *Mrs L. Hartley*

Take what quantity of fresh Beef you like, put it in a pot with some Slices of Butter, season it with pepper & Salt, a little Shalot or Garlic is good in it. bake it tender & whilst warm, beat it well in a Marble or Wooden Mortar with melted Butter & the fat it is baked in. put it very close down in pots, & when cold pour clarified Butter over it.

2 lb (900g) beef, lean brisket or stewing steak
4 oz (125g) butter   pepper and salt to taste
2 cloves garlic

Place all the ingredients in a small casserole and bake for 3 hours at gas mark 3, 325°F (170°C) until the meat is tender. Remove the beef, cut it into cubes and either mince finely, or grind in a blender or food processor together with the remaining stock, adding further seasoning if necessary.

While the meat is cooking, melt a further 2 oz (50g) of butter in a pan with half a cup of water, beat them together, then allow to cool, so that the clarified butter sets sufficiently firmly that the water may be poured off. Heat the butter gently until all the surplus water is driven off and the butter appears as a clear yellow oil without bubbles.

Finally press the meast paste down into sterilised dishes or jars, excluding all pockets of air, and seal by pouring a layer of the clarified butter across its surface.

Potted Cheese c.1865

1 lb of cheese well beaten in a mortar, add 2 ounces liquid butter, one glass of sherry & a little Cayenne, mace & salt. All to be well beaten together & put into a glass jar with a layer of lard at the top. Excellent with bread, or toast.

1 lb (450g) traditional cheese, mature for a good flavour
2 oz (50g) melted butter   1 glass (50 ml dry sherry)
small pinch of cayenne pepper and ground mace
½ tsp (2.5 ml) salt

211

Pound all the ingredients together using a mortar and pestle, or a food processor, until an extremely smooth paste is formed. Pack down into a jar, excluding all pockets of air, and keep covered in a cool place until used within the next 2–3 days. It is best eaten spread on hot toast.

Pickled Mushrooms   Mrs L. H.

When your Mushrooms are clean'd with a piece of fine flannel throw them into milk & water, then drain them well, put them in a pan with a little Salt thrown over them, & when you think they are enough lay them on a cloth to cool, when quite cold put them in a pickle of white wine vinegar, mace, white pepper & a little of their own Liquor, put a little Oil on top of your Bottles & tie them close down.

1 lb (450g) button mushrooms	1 tsp (15 ml) blade mace
2 tsp (10 ml) salt	1 tsp (5 ml) peppercorns
½ pt (250 ml) white wine vinegar	

Wash the mushrooms and place in a pan with the salt and 2 tbs (30 ml) water. Cover, bring slowly to the simmer, and allow to cook gently for some 15 minutes in their own juice before draining, retaining their liquor. In the meantime heat the vinegar and spices to the boil and allow to cool. Pack the mushrooms mixed with the spices into a sterilised jar, cover with the vinegar and a little of the mushroom liquor, and seal down tightly.

N.B. The remaining mushroom liquor heated with ½ pt (250 ml) milk produces a delicate mushroom soup.

To preserve Cherries in Brandy   Mrs L. Hartley

Pound & sift Lump Sugar thro' a Sieve & to every quart of Brandy put ½ lb of Sugar and let it dissolve. take Morrell Cherries, wipe them very clean & dry, cut off half the stems & lay them into a wide Jar one at a time & fill the Jar with the Brandy & tie it down with a Bladder.

This recipe too gives good results.

Index

Index